SOMETHING
LEFT TO LOSE

Personal Relations
and Survival among
New York's Homeless

SOMETHING LEFT TO LOSE

Personal Relations
and Survival among
New York's Homeless

GWENDOLYN A. DORDICK

Temple University Press
Philadelphia

Temple University Press, Philadelphia 19122
Copyright © 1997 by Temple University. All rights reserved
Published 1997
Printed in the United States of America

♾ The paper used in this book meets the requirements
of the American National Standard for Information Sciences—Permanence
of Paper for Printed Library Materials, ANSI Z39.48–1984

Text design by David denBoer

Library of Congress Cataloging-in-Publication Data
Dordick, Gwendolyn A., 1961–
    Something left to lose : personal relations and survival among New
York's homeless / Gwendolyn A. Dordick.
      p.   cm.
    Includes bibliographical references and index.
    ISBN 1-56639-513-5 (cloth : alk. paper). — ISBN 1-56639-514-3
(pbk. : alk. paper)
    1. Homeless persons—New York (State)—New York—Case studies.
2. Interpersonal relations—New York (State)—New York—Case studies.
I. Title.
HV4506.N6D67   1997
305.5′69—dc20   96-25094

Portions of Gwendolyn A. Dordick, "More Than Refuge: The Social World of
a Homeless Shelter," *Journal of Contemporary Ethnography* 24 (4), pp. 373–404,
copyright © 1996 by Sage Publications, are reprinted by permission of Sage
Publications.

for SETH

CONTENTS

PREFACE

I SPENT THE FIFTEEN MONTHS BETWEEN MAY 1990 and September 1991 with four groups of homeless people in New York City: inhabitants of a large bus terminal, the Station; residents of a shantytown, the Shanty; occupants of a large public shelter, the Armory; and clients of a small, church-run private shelter, the Private Shelter. Day after day I would visit, hanging out with the men and women who lived there, talking informally with individuals or small groups, watching and occasionally participating in the daily flow of life among the homeless. It was at different moments intriguing and dull, funny and heartbreaking, dangerous and routine.

I spent evenings capturing what I had observed in sets of field notes. I described sights and smells; wrote down circumstances and events; transcribed my conversations with individuals who had graciously allowed me to record them on cassette tapes. I filled page after page, a thousand or so in all, with the raw data of my experiences.

What follows is my attempt to make sense of those experiences, to document as best I can how the people I visited live. I have chosen to reproduce my respondents' syntax and slang word for word. I have done so not to call attention to their poverty or lack of education but rather to preserve their voices and to present their words and the rhythm of their expression with the same vividness that I was privileged to hear.

My greatest debt is, of course, to the people I met. I cannot adequately express my appreciation for their generosity in sharing their lives with a young, relatively privileged, and occasionally clumsy sociology graduate student. I miss many of them.

I also wish to thank those who helped me understand what I saw. My dissertation committee—Kim Hopper, Kathryn Neckerman, Brendan O'Flaherty, Allan Silver, and Herbert Gans—provided many thoughtful and insightful comments that helped clarify my ideas. I am especially indebted to Allan Silver and Herbert Gans for reading more proposal and manuscript drafts than I (or they) would like to remember. Their detailed comments on each draft encouraged me to work even harder. I owe special thanks to Herbert Gans, who challenged me and pushed me to push myself from the moment I set foot in the Columbia University Sociology Department.

Several others, both teachers and colleagues, have influenced and continue to influence my career. William Roy encouraged me to major in sociology while I was an undergraduate at UCLA. Bill Gibson, Clarence Lo, Patricia Greenfield, Patricia Lengermann, Steven Tuch, Ruth Wallace, Peter Blau, Eric Hirsch, Mark Stamey, Lewis Freeman, Anna Karpathakis, and Chris Toulouse have all influenced my development as a sociologist in many, often conflicting, ways. Special thanks are due Mark Mizruchi for consistently good—if not followed—advice; the late Olga Scarpeta for her inspiring optimism; and Fatimah Haneef for her bureaucratic prowess in actually wresting NIMH funds from Columbia's coffers. I thank my colleagues at Hamilton College—Frank Anechiarico, Alan Cafruny, Daniel Chambliss, Dennis Gilbert, Maurice Isserman, Cecelia Lawless, Elizabeth Regosin, and Paula Rust—for their positive outlook in the last stages of this project.

I thank Dave Giffen from the New York City Coalition for the Homeless, who graciously provided me with helpful information and the necessary documentation to do the research. I appreciate the financial support I received while in the field. I am indebted to Dr. Agnes Rupp from the National Institute of Mental Health for encouraging me to apply for the National Research Service Award (#1 F31 MH10269–01 BSR) and to the institute itself for granting it to me.

I am grateful to Michael Ames of Temple University Press for seeing promise in a dissertation that still needed much work and for encouraging me to write the book I wanted to write and to Jim Baumohl for his thoughtful critique. My copy editor, Elizabeth Johns, went above and beyond in her review of the manuscript, asking many valuable questions the answers to which have made this a better book. I wish to thank Donileen Loseke, editor of the *Journal of Contemporary Ethnography,* and two anonymous reviewers for comments and suggestions on an article concerning the Armory. I thank Sage Publications, publishers of the journal, for granting me permission to reprint portions of the article herein.

My friends and family gave me the emotional encouragement that sustained me through the sometimes painful fieldwork and writing of this book. To my parents, Ruth and Herbert Dordick, and my brother, Jonathan Dordick: Thank you for your love and support and, above all else, your honesty. To Seth: I dedicate this work to you.

PART I

On the Streets

CHAPTER ONE

"Your Word Is Your Bond": The Station

LOCATED ON TWO LARGE BLOCKS OF MANHAT-tan's West Side, the Station handles thousands of commuters who pass through it daily. On the main floors are bus terminals, ticketing windows, shops, and fast-food restaurants. Hot dog, pretzel, Italian ice, and incense vendors are scattered throughout the main floors of the Station and on surrounding streets. On the upper floors are more terminals and empty bus depots. Outside, the avenue is heavy with traffic, particularly taxicabs discharging and picking up passengers. Across the street are more shops; consumer electronics, check cashing services, liquor, and many kinds of food are available within a short distance. In a city of busy streets and congested avenues, the Station sits in the middle of one of the busiest.

Hell's Kitchen

You see, if you get hungry, you might kill someone. You might kill someone in order to eat. There are times that I've been out here that I'm so hungry, I felt like breakin' that window. Or if I walked by a restaurant, I felt like goin' in there and just takin' me somethin' 'cause I didn't have no money. If I went in there and asked somebody for somethin', nobody would give it to me, you understand. If I went in there and asked somebody for somethin', they would call the police and have me sent to jail.

Moses

Scattered among the daily commuters and summer visitors that I saw on my first visit to the Station were men, women, and "young ones," boys and girls of fifteen or sixteen whose guardians had kicked them out or who had run away from pasts they were reluctant to talk about. The first person to catch my eye was a frail legless man who was resting shirtless in a wheelchair in the shade. Next to him, against the cool concrete walls of the terminal building, was a small group of six men and women, all seeking relief from the summer heat. High temperatures, hot asphalt, and heavy traffic thickened the air and turned the corner into a sauna. A panhandler interrupted my gaze to ask for some change—"a donation," he called it. I dug into my pocket, but all I had was a pack of Newports, a token, a pen, and a small notebook. I offered him a cigarette. Behind him a woman vomited into a trash can. A man called over to me and asked if I needed any help. I introduced myself and told him I was a student doing a project on homeless people. He responded, "My name is Ron. I don't do crack, but I drink. Can I have a cigarette?" I handed one to him and lit it, taking one for myself. The tip of mine caught fire; I had lit the filter. Ron laughed. "I must be a little nervous," I said.

For Twin, a forty-seven-year-old Vietnam veteran, street life is "a very deep oppressor. An emotional, devastating, depressing, and humiliating thing." He knows, he explains, that he "cannot live among the rich." "I feel more comfortable down here," he says, "because I fit in." Twin had come to the Station from suburban Westchester County three days before I met him. Although he claims to "fit in" with the people at the Station, he refuses to sleep on the street or beg for money like many others there do. According to Twin:

> You never see me sleep in the street. I worked thirty-two years of my life. Went to prison in '85. I worked before you was born. I was brought up with a certain degree of independence through my parents. My daughter just graduated from St. John's University. And now all I need is two dollars to go and sit in a movie all night long. My pride is too good to beg. I don't want you to help me, Miss. I want you to understand me.

My first few days at the Station were less about understanding and more about what residents of the Station call "conversating." Many men and women were reluctant to talk to an outsider. Imagine their surprise and confusion when a tall, white, Jewish woman wearing long shorts, a Tom Petty tank top, and a baseball cap walked onto their congested corner claiming to be working on a research project. I was unsure what to say or how to discover what those at the Station kept referring to as "the real truth." I felt the difference between the life I was used to and street life.

For Moses, an older man in his mid-fifties who had been homeless about four months, such differences are clear:

> Living on the streets makes you do a lot of things that you wouldn't normally do. I've done a lot of things that I would not normally do because I'm comin' into

a different environment. I was brought up in the sub-
urbs; I always had jobs; I always had good relationships. Comin' into this environment I've done a lot
of things I said I wouldn't do.

"Getting by," surviving at the Station, Moses attests, requires homeless people to do things they "wouldn't nor-
mally do." Eating food discarded on the sidewalk, rummaging through trash, using makeshift toilets, sleeping in
one's clothes tightly grasping all one's belongings—all are
indignities that constitute the routine lives of the homeless
who live there. Moses explains:

There was some people that came along in a van and
just threw sandwiches on the street and I picked them
up and ate them. I was hungry and I never did it [be-
fore]. The guilt almost killed me 'cause I never done
anything like that and my pride kicked up. But my
stomach said, "Hey, listen, you better eat this food."
. . . A lot of times I go to sleep at night, and then when
I wake up, you know, I'm right here, faced with the
same thing. I say, "Another fucked up day"—you
know what I'm saying? As the days go on, as the
months go on, you get adjusted, conditioned, you
know how people are conditioned.

Surviving at the Station is a full-time job. The homeless
anguish over getting money, procuring food, and, most
important, protecting themselves in an uncertain and un-
forgiving environment. In due time, Moses claims, Twin
too will "get adjusted" and will "learn to sleep on the
street."

Sources of outside support for the people at the Station

are quite limited. According to sociologist Peter Rossi, "Homeless people have slipped through the loose weave of our existing social welfare safety nets."[1] Public assistance offers little. Benefits are meager and are available only to those who have an address and patiently enroll themselves on all the required lists. Even those who follow all the steps and make it onto the welfare rolls do not always receive their benefits.[2] Moses, for example, enrolled two months ago. According to Moses: "I haven't received anything. They give me the runaround." Most of those I spoke to received no public assistance.[3] Moses, like the others, is "pushed into doin' other things."

Opportunities for steady employment are scarce, in part because the demand for unskilled labor in New York City continues to decline.[4] In addition, the expansion of New York's informal economy has altered the geographic distribution of the remaining low-wage jobs that might still have been a source of employment for unskilled urban laborers. These jobs, however, have moved from the city to outlying areas.[5] To make matters worse, the jobs that do remain in the city are intermittent and hard to secure for homeless people who cannot provide a potential employer with an "acceptable" address. When employment does come, it is usually day to day. Such forms of work are often exploitative and undependable.

The homeless at the Station develop their own strategies to make money. According to Ron, "If you can't get a job or get on welfare, then you're pushed into doing other things, things that you never thought you would ever do." As Moses says, if you're tired enough, hungry enough, and cold enough, you will, in time, "hustle" in order to get by: "Hustling in the sense of surviving. Anything that I could do to get a meal and to have shelter, put it that way. I'm not saying one thing specifically. It could be panhandling, washing car windows, a variety of things. Hustling is to take care of oneself."

Almost anything can qualify as "hustling." Eating sandwiches that are discarded on the street, mustering the patience to get on welfare rolls, standing in line at a soup kitchen—all these are "hustling," as are panhandling; washing car windows; selling clothes, furniture, and other items on the street; pimping; prostitution; and drug dealing.

Panhandling is the most popular hustle at the Station. When it is time to "make the donuts," the homeless can be found canvasing the busy street for hours at a time, repeating catchy phrases such as "give Chucky a buck," and "we need donations." Sayjay and Joey's favorite spot is a check-cashing place opposite the Station. According to Sayjay, "We go over to the check-cashing place and we ask people for money when they come out. Sometimes they give you dollars."

The Station's central location is conducive to other hustles as well. Sometimes Sayjay and Raheem do chores— heavy cleaning and small carpentry work—at a nearby church in exchange for food and clothes. The homeless at the Station occasionally make money—usually ten dollars—by offering to participate in police line-ups. Others, such as William, make money by working for the hot-dog vendors, either washing their carts for five dollars apiece or carrying ice for them. A deaf-mute, William communicates with hand and body signals and facial gestures. After William showed me what he did to make money, he pointed to the sky and then plugged his nose. He repeated this gesture over and over again. Finally Sayjay explained that William was trying to tell me that he was "dead and stinkin'." (Pointing to the sky signified heaven and death while plugging his nose signified stinking.) According to Sayjay, it means "I ain't got nothin'."

Hustling, as the homeless at the Station understand it, bears strong resemblance to what sociologists David Snow and Leon Anderson term "shadow work." Defined as "compensatory, non-wage labor subsistence strategies," shadow work involves "recognition and exploitation of whatever resources and unofficial markets happen to be available whenever a few dollars are needed."[6] The concept of shadow work is intended to differentiate activities like panhandling and scavenging from itinerant labor, but this distinction is not shared by those I studied. Whether they wash a hot-dog cart for a vendor or "sing for their supper," the homeless see themselves as simply working. Hustling encompasses both "legitimate" and "shadow" work. In exhorting themselves and one another to hustle, the homeless appropriate the mainstream American ideal of self-reliance.[7]

An ethic of self-reliance informs accounts of hustling at the Station. The men and women who live there believe that they are providing for themselves. For them, panhandling is work, not a passive dependence on outsiders. Given their hard circumstances, many at the Station take considerable pride in their ability to get by. "I may be homeless, but I'm not helpless. I believe in myself," says Ron. Streams of travelers make the Station an attractive locale for hustling and also make it relatively safe. Day or night, the Station, like the avenue outside, is alive and congested. The continuous presence of people makes it safer than more secluded locations—such as abandoned buildings or dark subway stations—where other homeless people live.

Late at night the situation is somewhat different. With

the exception of Grandma Dynamite, an elderly woman afforded special privileges by Station police officers, the homeless are not permitted to sleep in the public areas of the Station or on the street corners outside. At night they take refuge in empty bus depots or upper floors removed from the hustle and bustle below. Many of the men and women who live at the Station sleep together on the seventh floor. Makeshift beds are built from discarded wooden fruit and vegetable crates and large pieces of cardboard. Clothing, blankets, and newspapers cushion hard surfaces and provide some warmth. Though there is some safety in numbers, stories of violent acts and even murder are common. On an early visit to the Station, I found a roped-off stairwell where a homeless woman had been stabbed to death the night before.

Outside authority, a combination of Station and city police, constrain but do not control the lives of the homeless at the Station. Station police, though vigilant in regulating the activity of the homeless during the day, rarely bother them at night. Discretionary policing is the norm: rules are enforced and penalties distributed according to each officer's judgment. During morning and evening rush hours, or when the chief of police is making an inspection, Station residents, specifically those who happen to be outside hustling at the time, are herded back and forth across the street by the police in their attempt to secure an even flow of pedestrian traffic through the Station. According to one officer: "It's a game, man. You got to play the game. That's it."

At first, the police had no idea who I was or why I was hanging around the Station. One afternoon, very early in my research, I was sitting against the terminal building talking with some people when an elderly gentleman approached to ask, "How much for a blow job?" and he pulled out five dollars. I replied that I was not for sale, showing him my university identification to corroborate my explanation for being there. He turned completely red and retreated. Homeless witnesses to the incident laughed. A police officer also saw what had happened. Grabbing me, he took me around the corner to ask who "the hell" I was and what "the hell" I was doing. Once again I produced my I.D. and explained myself. He shook his head several times and told me I was "crazy." He tried to persuade me to leave, arguing that "these people are dangerous." I listened patiently, promising him and the three other officers who had joined in that I would be careful. For a few more days they continued to urge me to leave, but eventually they left me alone.

The police are not always so benign. According to Ron, one night a resident was kicked by a Station cop:

> You know, you should come out here with a camera and take some real shots. You know, you may have an invalid laying down here. He's got problems and the [Station] cops will come up and kick him. Like he's an animal with no rights. They will also arrest and overcharge you. In other words, when I say overcharge you, if you get arrested, they may put another charge on you, and you won't know it until you get to court.

According to Moses, "The police move people from corner to corner. They arrest people for nothin'. They arrest people for being homeless." The police may also deny the men and women who live at the Station equal justice. According to Ron:

When you try to go to make a complaint, they don't want to hear about it. Or you go in there and make a complaint, they have you sittin' in there all day for nothin'. They tell you they don't have time. Now, if I had a suit and tie and walked in there with a briefcase and I said I want to make a formal complaint and told them I was robbed or whatever, then they would react.

The discretionary power of the police at the Station, a power very much like that observed by sociologist Egon Bittner in a study of police on skid row, leads some of the homeless to learn to work with the authorities.[8] The police, they explain, are most concerned with the flow of traffic in and around the Station. By agreeing to "make themselves scarce" during rush hours, by "playing the game," the homeless cultivate relationships with individual police officers. Ron, for example, has developed a relationship with a police lieutenant. He says the officer told him, "Look, if one of these cops out here abuses somebody or harasses somebody, take the number and let me see it." Like Bittner's police officers, those at the Station are more interested in "keeping the peace" between the Station's diverse clientele than in piling up arrests for the petty crimes. Where abuse exists, it tends to focus on homeless individuals who have not cultivated good relationships with the police. These relationships have their costs, however. By avoiding popular areas during rush hour, the homeless are forced to refrain from panhandling and other such activities during the time when they would be most profitable.

There is little privacy at the Station. Day and night, the homeless who live there are in view of one another, police, and travelers. Secluded areas are regarded as dangerous, and the homeless prefer familiar parts of the Station where others can be found. Public restrooms—another advantage of the Station—do allow men and women to take care of their personal hygiene in relative privacy. Those who own more than the clothes on their backs can also use the restroom sinks to do laundry. Coin-operated lockers at the Station offer limited and expensive private space to store belongings. Some residents also keep their clothing in lockers in public shelters. Most, however, simply carry their possessions with them.

The Clique on the Corner

These people, when I got down here, these people reached out to me because they knew, they already knew what it was like. They're not afraid to help their fellow man. As soon as I got down here I met Ron and the fellows and they didn't push me away. I mean I didn't know where to go, I didn't know where to eat, I didn't know where to sleep. They just invited me right in. And ever since then at least I've been healthy, and I've been clean since I've met them.

Moses

Outside on the avenue, homeless men and women gather, laughing and talking. Some "conversate"—that is, they have intimate and private conversations that are not to be interrupted—while others sit quietly watching as people pass. This is "hanging out," the most common activity of street life, a way of passing stretches of unstructured time. Like the men and women I met, I would often sit against the building or on the sidewalk across the street and watch people for hours, often speaking with no one. Hanging out gave me the opportunity to learn about the people and environment I was "visiting."[9]

Hanging out does more than kill time. It enables men and women at the Station to learn their milieu and to maintain familiarity with a constantly changing environment. People at the Station come and go. Potential friends and enemies present themselves on a daily basis. Each time I visited the Station I saw both familiar and new faces. One day, for example, I met Rakeem. "I'm the young one, I'm the baby. Me and my mother don't get along. We have fights, so I leave home. You understand?" Rakeem is a boastful fifteen-year-old boy. "I got my people to watch my back only when I need them," he bragged to me and Sayjay. Sayjay laughed, "He's got the biggest mouth on the block." That was the first and last time I saw Rakeem. In an environment as large as the Station, one so public and so central to the flow of people throughout the metropolitan area, there will always be new homeless people. As D.C. claims, "Every day you meet someone new." Sizing these people up is an essential part of hanging out. Staying current in a fast-paced environment requires an almost continuous presence.

One way in which the residents of the Station make their environment more familiar and secure is through nicknames. As one becomes a regular, one acquires more and more of them. One day Joey was referred to as Quant, short for Quantity, because he collected so much money panhandling on that particular day. Another day he was called Doo-Doo because he collected little to nothing. And on another day he was Buckwheat, a character from the Little Rascals, because he woke up with his hair sticking straight up. Sayjay is known as Pitbull because of his boisterous and sometimes aggressive demeanor. One day, however, several people called him Brooklyn for reasons he could not ascertain. Ron told me that his nickname was Cisco, although I never heard anyone use it. Some residents refer to Ron as Romeo because of his flirtatious manner. I was addressed as the Secret Agent, the Federal Agent, or Agent 000, names that insinuated that I was working undercover despite my openness about what I was doing. My role at the Station was best summed up by Gypsy, who said, "You down [you belong] in your own way." Like gossip and hanging out, nicknames enable the homeless, like other social groups, to establish boundaries between the familiar and the unfamiliar. To give another a nickname is a way of expressing a knowledge or an understanding of that person, or at least to say that they are regular enough—or, as Gypsy puts it, "around"—to deserve a nickname. Those with nicknames, including myself, can be said to have something of an insider status. In an environment that is full of strangers, they denote familiarity.

Over and above what appears to the outsider to be "effortless sociability"[10] among regulars are closer ties that bind some residents of the Station into groups. Over time I could discern two distinct and stable groups, each occupying one of the two large blocks on which the Station sits. That is, I began to notice both through direct observation and through a review of my field notes that the same individuals could consistently be found together. Although these two groups occupy separate blocks and are ethnically and racially different—one is predominantly Puerto Rican and the other predominantly African American—they are not overtly antagonistic. Ron, Joey, Sayjay, Raheem, and Rico, the predominantly black group whom I refer to as the "clique," are the focus of my analysis. The choice of which group to focus on was unavoidable. As I do not speak Spanish, I could learn little from the Puerto Rican group. Furthermore, Ron was the first to befriend me when I came to the Station. His acceptance and guidance, in the end, allowed me to get closer to the men in the clique.

Ron

Ron, a man in his mid-thirties, is articulate, strong-willed, and unafraid to voice opinions and beliefs to the men in the clique, Station residents, or the police. Ron tries in his conversations to articulate the injustices of street life: "When people come through [the Station], the first thing they say to themselves is that we are derelicts, winos, and cutthroats. . . . The bottom line is that if you're homeless, you don't have a voice; you're nothin'. That's the bottom line. You don't have a voice; you're not a productive part of society." His pride and self-respect are evident. He sees himself as "an inspiration to other homeless people," wanting them to "do something with their lives." Ron's hair is short and well kept. He is clean shaven and dresses appropriately for the hot summer weather. When I first met him, he was wearing a pair of cream slacks, a light blue buttoned-down shirt, and a pair of clean sneakers. On other occasions he wore shorts and polo shirts. Ron's concern over appearance is evident: his clothes are clean and his outfits well coordinated. "I may be homeless, but I don't have to look homeless," he explains.

Raheem

Raheem has known Ron for about two and a half years. He is twenty-four and has been "on the streets" for eight years. He finds it "exciting." He has had several jobs in the area but is currently unemployed. Raheem has problems with his eyes. Often, in the morning, his vision is so blurred that he cannot see directly in front of him. Raheem explains, "I can't see across the street. I need an eye operation. Suddenly, a few months ago, I just woke up in the morning and couldn't see. It was blurry. They gave me something to take. . . . But I haven't really been takin' them like I should be takin' them." Raheem needs to take two medications that a doctor prescribed, but his prescriptions have run out. Raheem refers to the men in the Station clique as "a family." He frequently boasts of their general solidarity and willingness to sacrifice. When I asked Raheem if he would help Sharon, who visits but is not a member of the group, he replied, "Well, I don't really know Sharon all that well, but I would help her." But for Raheem and other group members, solidarity and self-sacrifice are maxims more easily honored as ideals than in practice. During our conversation I noticed a woman doubled over a trash can, looking sick. I asked Raheem if we should help. He shook his head and continued our conversation. Raheem is approximately the same height and build as Ron. He is clean shaven, keeps his hair short, and usually wears a pair of shorts, a T-shirt, and a pair of sneakers. Raheem lacks Ron's wardrobe. Though not as concerned about his appearance as Ron, Raheem is neither sloppy nor unkempt.

Sayjay

Sayjay, in his mid-thirties like Ron, has been in the clique for about a year. Originally from Virginia, for a time he worked as a welder in New Jersey. He met a woman from New York, quit his job, and moved in with her. When the relationship ended, Sayjay found himself jobless and homeless. He lived for a few months in Harlem 2, a public shelter for homeless men. Now he lives at the Station, using the shelter only to store clothing and do his laundry. At the time I first met him, Sayjay was wearing a pair of sweatpants and a T-shirt. Later that day, as evening approached, he changed into a pair of shorts, claiming that it would help when he panhandled because people would be unable to resist his "pretty legs." Sayjay is clean shaven and shorter than both Ron and Raheem. His teeth are crooked and yellowed. He speaks with a slight southern accent and has a loud, infectious laugh.

Joey

Joey is the smallest and most disheveled member of the clique. Also in his mid-thirties, he looks older than Ron and Sayjay. He is a little shorter than Sayjay and much thinner. His hair is unkempt (hence the nickname Buckwheat), his face unshaven, and his clothes baggy. His disheveled appearance, however, is an asset when it comes to panhandling, a job he does well. According to Sayjay, "Joey's good to panhandle with because they look at this little skinny guy, undernourished, and say that they got to get this guy something."[11] Joey drinks. He has been in and out of detox for the last four years. He has been at the Station for four months. During my visits there, Joey went into detox only to return to an environment that does not directly encourage drinking but does not provide strong reasons to abstain. According to Rico, Joey needs to "get away" if he is to stop drinking.

Rico

Also in his thirties, Rico is the only nonblack member of the clique. Even though his cousin hangs out on the Puerto Rican block, Rico chooses to spend most of his time with Ron, Joey, Sayjay, and Raheem because he has "more fun" with them. Rico likes to have fun. Every time he sees Ron or Joey, or any other members of the clique, he asks if this is "where the party is." The men often tease Rico about his lack of seriousness. However, in more somber moments, Rico can be quite serious about his situation. According to Rico, "I'm just homeless in the street and acting stupid. All I do is party, sing, and talk. The same thing we do every night. It's no picnic."

Ron, Raheem, Joey, Rico, and Sayjay—the clique—are virtually inseparable. They work together, hustling to obtain money and food. They eat meals together. They go on outings—to local soup kitchens, to movies, to free outdoor concerts in a nearby park. And they sleep together, either in the empty depots with the other homeless residents or in one of the all-night movie theaters located near the Station. On rare occasions when they are not together, they usually know where to find one another. When they do not, it is a matter of great concern. They worry that a missing clique member may have fallen victim to violence or been arrested. I often saw clique members canvassing the Station in search of a member whose whereabouts were unknown.

Most of the time the men in the clique are together, therefore, and most of that time is spent hanging out. The men gossip about what is going on within the clique and around them—who in the Station was arrested, who fell sick, and, in one instance, who was murdered. They also pass the day by telling stories of one another's antics the night before, including Joey's excessive drinking, by commenting on people going by, horsing around with each other, and flirting with women, both homeless ones and others.

Although the substance of their gossip is particular to their environment, when they are hanging out the men in the clique are quite similar to workers huddled around an office water cooler, to regulars sidled up at a neighborhood bar, or, in fact, colleagues milling about at an academic convention. What makes the homeless distinctive is that there is no protected space or time for such activities and that they do it all the time. Gossip provides the men in the clique with both a shared history and a common understanding of the events that transpire around them. Their experiences together are the material of their gossip. "It is like kicking about what happened last night," proclaims Gypsy. In talking with one another—"conversating" is their term—they discourage talk of life prior to being on the street. "Everybody has a sob story," the men explain. What history appears in conversation is a past the men have together, a past whose nearly constant recounting contributes to the solidarity of the clique.

In addition to hanging out and gossiping, the men sing together. Ron writes songs; Sayjay, Raheem, Rico, and Joey join in performing them. Ron says he has written over one hundred songs. According to Sayjay, Ron often goes off for long periods to a nearby park with a pencil and paper to write. (Even then, the others know where he is.) One of Ron's songs, clearly the most popular, is a rap song titled "Get Off the Crack." When the group performed it during one of my visits, other homeless residents of the Station came over to join in, clapping on the beat and singing the chorus. Other songs are more blues-like in tone: one extols the virtue of believing only in oneself; another proclaims the promise of children. On these Sayjay, Raheem, Rico, and Joey sing harmony while Ron sings the melody. Below are the words to one of Ron's songs that the men in the clique would sing frequently:

> The time has come for you and me
> To teach the children, yes, what ought to be.
> We've had our share of ups and downs
> Let's face the truth, they don't respect us now.
> > [*Refrain*] Oh, take the time and show them how
> > We can make them different now.
> > The road they choose is up to us.
> > We have to sacrifice our love.
> I heard some people say just the other day
> Why don't we take the children and put them all
> > away.
> Heed your heart and teach them well
> Don't make excuses because you ought to care.
> > [*Refrain*]
> When a child is born we try to teach them well
> That everything in life isn't always fair.
> Take a look around at the kids today
> But we don't even care.
> > [*Refrain*]

Some of Ron's songs are more personal expressions. In one, written for his daughter, he apologizes for being unable to be with her at Christmas.

Ron's songs express three distinct levels of social life at the Station. The rap song demonstrates the sociability of the homeless community at the Station. The blues songs show the greater solidarity among the men in the clique. And finally the song written for his daughter displays his individuality, by which I mean a life, if not a home, separate from that at the Station. Ron's songs reflect his ambivalence toward group life there. While they contribute to the solidarity between members of the clique, the songs are for him—both in the solitary process of writing them and in the message of at least some of them—a way of expressing an individuality that is difficult to maintain and nurture in an environment as public as that of the Station.

A Man's World

The Station in general and the clique in particular are a man's world. Although women can often be found "hanging out" with the clique, they are not seen as members. Many, like Angel and Sharon, spend their days at the Station but their nights elsewhere.

Angel, a white woman in her early twenties, lives in a nearby home for the mentally ill. Her mannerisms and speech are slurred, abbreviated, and childlike. When she is angry she stamps her feet, screaming and crying like a child throwing a temper tantrum. Angel is a source of income for the men at the Station. She collects Supplemental Security Income (SSI). When she visits the Station, the men expect her to buy them beer. They have sex with her as well. According to Rico, "She hangs out around here and sleeps with everybody." When I asked if he had had sex with Angel, Rico hesitated for a moment and then replied, "It's been done." He then told me that she was two months' pregnant, although not by him.

Sharon, a thin black woman in her early thirties, is wise to the false promises made by the men at the Station. Even something as seemingly innocent as a glance is immediately met with resistance. "Don't look at them!" she advised me during one visit, quickly averting her eyes from a stranger's unwelcome glance. Although she likes to hang out at the Station during the day, she spends her nights in a women's shelter away from the men—in particular Ron and Raheem, whom she refers to, only half joking, as "the horny brothers." Women like Sharon and Angel, with more to fear and less to fall back on in the sometimes violent world of the street, choose to sleep elsewhere whenever possible.

My initial affiliation with Ron, and subsequently the men of the clique, restricted my contact with the women at the Station. The men were possessive of both my time and attention. Additionally, the more I became one of the boys, the more at least some of the women grew suspicious of my motives, remaining cautious and distant. I tried, with limited success, to talk with women alone, away from the men. But privacy is a scarce commodity at the Station. One must literally "step off the corner" in order to carry on a private conversation. Not surprisingly, no one would leave. When that failed, I tried to talk with them in pairs or in groups of three or more, hoping that this would dispel their fear. On many occasions, they told me outright that they didn't want to talk to me and walked away. Others simply turned and walked in the other direction when they saw me approaching. Most of the women, however, did not run away but ignored me, rarely allowing me to probe past informal conversation. I learned from Sharon that I was seen as competition. She told me that many women felt the men were interested in me only because I had money or because I was a white woman.

This problem came to a head with Angel. One day Ron, Rico, Sayjay, and a few other Station residents were gathered in front of a small grocery store talking with her. I approached them and said hello. Ron put his arm on my shoulder and said, "Here's my girl," a flirtatious phrase he used often. When Angel heard this she became furious, yelling at Ron for having a "girlfriend" and for "cheating" on her. Ron and the others tried to calm her down by assuring her that I was not Ron's girlfriend. I joined in, telling her that I was a student working on a school project and that I had a boyfriend and it was not Ron. She snapped back that I was "a liar," that I was "fucking lying." The more I tried to talk to her the angrier she got. Finally I simply left, leaving Ron and the others to calm her down and repair the damage I had done.

Despite her angry protests to the contrary, Angel is not Ron's girlfriend. In fact, the constant companionship of the men in the clique makes one-on-one sexual relationships almost impossible. Their obligation to remain together leaves little room or time for love. "When I love you, I love you to death," claims Sayjay. "I'm used to having a girlfriend, but I don't have one here." The men in the clique do not have steady girlfriends, but they most certainly have sex. According to Sayjay, "If there are boots to be smoked, they're gonna be smoked." This translates into, "If there's sex to be had, then it will be had." At the Station, men and women engage in brief, often one-time sexual encounters in circumstances of limited privacy. According to Moses, "There's a lot of screwing, and people do it anywhere they can. They do it in the back, in the bathrooms, in cars in alleyways, and in cellars and basements. Anywhere they can." These encounters carry with them few expectations. The women who sleep with the men in the clique have no greater relationship with them than other familiar residents at the Station.

Unfortunately, these one-night sexual encounters can have disastrous consequences for the women. Pregnancy is common on the streets. The fear of having a baby, and having to care for a baby, forces women to take drastic measures. According to Moses:

> It's one thing being homeless, but pregnant and homeless? Some women have their babies right out here; others get rid of them. Some of them get an abortion. Some of them abort theirself by sticking hangers up their vaginas. I've seen that myself. This young girl didn't want a baby and she stuck a hanger up her vagina. She had to go to the hospital. They managed to keep her alive. She went through a lot of trouble. They had to sew her up and stuff. There definitely needs to be birth control. But then a special thing comes into play: the religious thing, be fruitful and multiply. A lot of women believe in God and just, you know, believe in whatever happens, happens. But a lot of young girls are scared because they never faced it. So right away they want to get rid of it, so they do the first thing that they can do.

Moses' statement captures the incomprehensibility of having a baby on the streets. To make matters worse, the physical danger these women face when utilizing a crude method of abortion such as Moses describes is complicated by "the religious thing," the belief that what they are doing is wrong.

The men at the Station blame their poverty for their lack of relationships. The responsibilities of a relationship with a woman are, they explain, difficult for men on the street. According to Moses:

Well, I have a lot of girls that like me, but I don't really feel it's right to start a relationship. I mess with a few girls just to maintain my manhood. I don't really feel it's right to take a woman out here and try to have a relationship, a street relationship, because you have to look out for one another. A woman might have to do some things that she don't like, that she never did. She gonna have to prostitute. And the man might have to sell a few crafts and have to hustle in some type of way to make sure she has her cigarettes, her menstruation pads, and a place to take a bath. It's about hustling, it's about taking care of one another. It's hard on the emotional stuff. You have other men that can come up and has a lot more to offer your woman and she might turn her back on you. Then it becomes a hassle because you have to preserve your honor, you end up fightin'.

For Moses, and for the men in the clique, the obligation of a man and a woman to take care of one another is difficult to sustain in abject poverty.

Running in Place, Together

We don't deny nobody.

Sayjay

Members of the clique help each other "get by." One way is by singing Ron's songs for money. After Ron, Raheem, Joey, Rico, and Sayjay perform a song, Joey takes off his cap and parades back and forth asking the audience for a "donation." Each performance usually brings in a few dol-

lars in change. The men in the clique also panhandle together. Although Joey is often chosen to be the one to ask
for the money because of his disheveled and undernourished appearance, the others are usually nearby encouraging passers-by to give money. This would not seem to be
the most optimal strategy: the men would most likely make
more money by dividing up and panhandling separately.
However, there is safety in numbers. Panhandling in isolation, like sleeping in isolation, can be dangerous. Furthermore, the men in the clique, with the exception of
Ron, hate to be alone.

In panhandling the men in the clique abide by rules that
apply throughout the Station and in other settings. In a
detailed analysis of the social and practical mechanics of
panhandling in New Haven, Connecticut, Yale student
Brandt Goldstein found businesslike norms prevalent
among panhandling "regulars" on a city street: "Three
norms, in particular, reflected the regulars' intense interest in preserving the favorable panhandling conditions in
the York district: (1) respecting pedestrians, (2) maintaining minimum distances between panhandlers, and (3)
honoring existing claims to territory."[12] Similar rules apply at the Station. D.C., a relative newcomer to the Station, was admonished by Sayjay after he got into an argument with a man whom he accidentally grazed with the
tip of his cigarette. The angered man enlisted the aid of a
police officer, who reprimanded D.C. Sayjay yelled at
D.C., telling him that "you never involve a cop." For
Sayjay, not only did D.C. initiate a quarrel with a pedestrian but as a consequence allowed the situation to escalate to the point that the police were involved, thus calling unnecessary attention to their activities. Panhandlers
at the Station are also conscious of territory. Once an in-

dividual or a group has occupied a spot, others are expected to stay away.

Singing requires cooperation within the group. Although Ron writes the songs, he could not perform them
without the others singing harmony. They usually perform
at the terminal entrance. The rap-like song "Get Off the
Crack" is their biggest crowd pleaser. Its strong avowal of
a drug-free life is a proven money getter among passers-by
sympathetic to its message:

> Green top, red top, white ones too.
> This a song I'm gonna sing for you.
> > [*Refrain*] Get off the crack.
> > Get off the crack.
> > Get off the crack.
> > Get off the crack.
> One, two, three, let's go.
> It's like nothin' you ever seen.
> You sell your soul and pawn your diamond ring.
> And once you got it and start to feel the rush.
> That's when you know, my God, you just can't get
> > enough.
> > [*Refrain*]
> It's a monster hanging on your back.
> You try to shake it, but it keeps comin' back.
> And when you think that it's finally gone away.
> It sticks you up and rides you every day.
> > [*Refrain*]
> Seen some young girls just the other night.
> Oh, yeah.
> Standin' in the hall.
> Where.
> And blowin' on the pipe.

They said they like it, they like the rush.
They sold their body for only five bucks.
  [*Refrain*]

The zeal with which the men sing and panhandle is in-
spired by a belief in the kindness of strangers. They would
not continue these activities unless they were profitable.
Residents brag of monetary gifts, embellishing the amount
of the gift and the generosity of the benefactor. One such
story assumed a folkloric quality. Raheem had fallen asleep
outside the Station. He was vaguely aware that someone was
tucking a bill into his pocket and remembered thinking, before he nodded off to sleep once more, that it was probably
a one-dollar bill. When he awoke he reached into his pocket
and to his surprise and great pleasure pulled out a ten-dollar
bill. Raheem's story was repeated by clique members on
several occasions. Joey told me that a "guy" gave Raheem
twenty dollars; Sayjay said some "dude" just gave Raheem
fifty dollars. In the end, all that mattered was their belief,
whether grounded in reality or not, that people will give
generous sums of money even when they are not solicited.
The story portrays strangers as good and helpful, and it was
told over and over again, the amount of money and the
kindness of the stranger growing with each narration. Stories about other such kind gestures—musicians giving them
free tickets to a show, ushers looking the other way as they
sneak into a movie theater, strangers inviting them to "stay
for a month"—were also commonly repeated.

These stories play an important role in the lives of clique
members. Panhandlers must deal with the almost constant
rejection of passers-by. Blasé New Yorkers, inured to begging on the street, often walk by without looking. Short of
taking a more aggressive strategy—badgering pedestrians

until they produce some change to get rid of them—clique members remain relatively sedate, merely ribbing passers-by who fail to make "donations." Like salesmen making "cold calls,"[13] the homeless avoid discouragement by holding out the hope, however fanciful, of "landing a big one." Such a hope manifests itself in the belief that people are kind and in stories that demonstrate their generosity.

Cooperation is evident also in obtaining food. On many occasions clique members hustle reluctant restaurant employees and street vendors into giving them food. One summer day Joey, Sayjay, Rico, D.C., and I decided to visit the *U.S.S. Kennedy,* a Navy ship that had docked in New York for a few days. On the way, we paused outside a liquor store. Sayjay entered and moments later emerged with a bottle of beer and a couple of sodas. Farther down the block D.C. talked a bread delivery man into giving him a fresh loaf. Joey asked D.C. for the bread. He split it open and walked into a restaurant. He came out a few minutes later with sliced tomatoes and lettuce inside the bread. Joey and Rico then walked over to a hot-dog vendor and after much debate talked him into giving them a hot dog. In the end, they had put together a sandwich. In approaching each of these people, the men relied on a mixture of charm and perseverance. Intimidation, as far as I could tell, did not play a role; the men smiled and laughed through each encounter. Good relationships with neighborhood merchants have long-term value for the homeless at the Station and elsewhere. Like salespeople working a client base, they push hard but not too hard. This is not to say that a subtle form of intimidation was not at work. The merchants might give to the men simply in order to be left alone and to avoid a scene. The merchants are certainly aware, however, that on another day the homeless will return.

Routinely, a member of the clique brings food back to the Station to share with other members. Throughout the day and night, clique members make what they call "trips" for food. Fried chicken, chicken and rice, pizza, hot dogs, and sandwiches make up much of their diet. For example, on one trip Ron purchased a turkey sandwich. He shared it with Sayjay and Joey, whom he found sitting outside the main terminal. Raheem joined them after they had finished the sandwich. Ron immediately reassured him that he would be the first to get food next time. Raheem shrugged his shoulders and told Ron, "It's all right; I'll wait until the next trip. On the next trip let's get chicken." Cigarettes, beer, and wine are procured and shared in a similar manner. Resources at the Station are liberally shared among clique members. As Raheem says, "If one person has money, and he buys food with that money, he buys for everybody."

"Everybody" usually means members of the clique, although occasionally other residents of the Station are included in the distribution of resources. Ron and Sayjay bought a box of crackers and generously shared them with Grandma Dynamite, Sharon, and Gypsy. Even those relatively new to the Station are not always left out. William, for example, had purchased some beer and was sharing it with Sayjay, Joey, and Rico. George, a newcomer from Louisiana, asked for some. Sayjay poured him a cup. A few minutes later, George asked for another cup. This time, however, Sayjay hesitated. "It's not mine to give," he said, pointing to William. George approached William and asked him for more beer. William nodded yes, and Sayjay poured another cup despite the fact that neither man was familiar with George.

Although sharing may extend beyond clique boundaries, it differs within and outside the clique. Within the clique, members simply expect a share of the resources: they need not ask. Witness how Raheem, having missed a meal, was reassured by Ron—without prompting—that he would be the first to get food on the next trip. Outside the clique, asking is required. As Sayjay says, "We don't deny nobody." Resources are not offered outside the clique, but they are often—not always, as Sayjay suggests— provided for those who ask. The decision not to deny outsiders maximizes the potential sources of aid in the event of need. In a world of unsteady and meager resource flows, broad sharing networks provide the greatest possible assurance that someone somewhere will have food. Even though William is not part of the clique, he can be asked for beer. Much like the job seekers in a study of a completely different environment, the homeless at the Station are keenly aware of the "strength of weak ties."[14]

The greatest expectations in terms of sharing fall upon clique members. Within the clique notions of personal property are, at least in the ideal, very limited. Through a practice that I term "collective sharing"—to distinguish it from sharing between pairs of individuals—resources technically in the possession of one clique member are assumed to belong to all of them. The strong collective orientation of the clique is demonstrated by the functioning of its "bank." On different days I heard individual clique members refer to one another as the "bank." The "bank," as the clique understands it, is the resident who is responsible for holding their money. Clique members are supposed to turn over money to the "bank" and are permitted to draw from it when they need funds. For example, Joey asked Ron, who is usually the "bank," if he could have some money to buy beer. Ron reached into his pocket and pulled out five dollars. He gave Joey two dollars and put the remaining three back in his pocket. When Joey returned he gave Ron the change.

The "bank" functions as the clique's pool of funds. Daily totals fluctuate considerably, and often the "bank" is empty. It never contains large sums of money. Its existence, however, raises questions concerning how the homeless get and save their money and how they spend it. Money from singing and panhandling is earned collectively, and money for food is spent collectively. Such collective activity has the deliberate effect of minimizing the kinds of complaints regarding equity that are almost inevitable in such cooperative relationships. However, individual deposits and withdrawals do exist and can be a source of considerable tension. In addition, Ron's sense that he contributes more to the clique than he receives also undermines group solidarity. Ron, who writes the songs, believes that the men in the clique "drag him down." Why, he argues, should he split the profits with the others? Ironically, Joey—the principal panhandler—does not complain like Ron that "people are taking advantage" of him.

Clique members also watch out for one another every day. Once Raheem fell asleep outside in the hot sun. Concerned that he would dehydrate, Sayjay woke Raheem up and suggested that it would be better for him to sleep upstairs or at least in a shaded area. Drinking too much can also cause dehydration. On another day Sayjay worried because Joey had drunk too much the night before and wanted a beer before he had had anything to eat. Sayjay did not allow Joey to drink any beer until he ate.

The men in the clique must also protect one another from potential enemies. Although the presence of passers-by makes the Station somewhat safer than more secluded areas, such as subway stations or abandoned buildings, it is difficult to distinguish between friends and enemies. It is also difficult to keep one's enemies away; they have a right to be in public spaces like the Station. Protecting oneself requires effort. Gypsy knowingly says, "Never run your enemy away. Keep them close so they can't hurt you. Buy them a drink, give them a cigarette."

Unfortunately, keeping one's enemies "close" is not a foolproof strategy. One day George, a relative unknown, became aggressive, frequently interrupting Raheem during a comic imitation of Richard Pryor. This exasperated both clique members and other residents. Rico, in particular, was furious and told George to be quiet and stop interrupting. The two men started screaming at each other. George walked away; Rico followed. Sayjay and Raheem grabbed Rico, but George told them to let Rico go so they could fight. Several other residents then grabbed George, holding him back as well. After several minutes of pleading, Sayjay and Raheem calmed both men down, and they promised not to fight. But later, when Raheem resumed his characterization of Richard Pryor, George suddenly reappeared and began shouting obscenities at Rico. Rico rose and marched over to George, but instead of hitting him he turned his back on George, bowed his head, and said several times, "I'm offering you my back." Unbeknownst to Rico, however, George was brandishing the jagged remains of a glass bottle. Raheem yelled to Rico, "He's got a bottle," and Rico quickly turned around. But before Rico could retaliate, George ran away. This incident demonstrates the importance of having allies. Raheem's warning saved Rico considerable physical harm and may even have saved his life. That

Rico, a much-venerated street fighter, needed the warnings of his companions to avert harm is testament to the importance of others in providing protection at the Station.

This incident also demonstrates one particular danger of life at the Station: the continuous influx of newcomers who may not always play by the rules. In turning his back on George, Rico demonstrated his expectations regarding how people should act at the Station or at least about how people should fight. In effect, what Rico was saying to George was, If you're going to hit me, then hit me. But if you hit me in the back, you're not fighting fair. However, in this environment one cannot count on others to meet one's expectations.

One day I learned how vulnerable I was without the support of the clique. Vet, a man in his late forties and an outsider to the Station, had been drinking. I was standing alone, leaning against an iron gate across from the pedestrian traffic of the Station, when he approached me, told me his name, and asked me for some money. His speech was badly slurred, and he wavered back and forth as he spoke. Following my usual practice of not giving money, I offered to buy him a cup of coffee.[15] Vet, however, replied that he didn't want coffee and started to tell me how much he liked me. I tried to change the subject, but he ignored me and continued to escalate his advances. He put his hand on my waist and told me that he wanted to "make love," and then he tried to kiss me. I pushed him away and told him to leave me alone. Angered by my response, he slammed me against the gate and started to yell, "Get the fuck out of here, get the fuck out. I'm gonna fuck you up and eat your pussy." I pushed him away and started to run. He stumbled after me. His yelling attracted

Ron and Sayjay, who came up and told him to leave me alone. Vet became even more agitated and repeatedly punched his hand against the iron gate, screaming that he was going to "fuck me up." Ron eventually calmed him down.

Thus the most important protection that the men in the clique provide one another is company. The homeless person alone is more vulnerable to attack from other homeless and from outsiders. As a group of five who travel together, the men in the clique clearly deter others from preying upon them. While overt acts of protection are rare, or seem trivial to the outsider, Ron, Sayjay, Raheem, Rico, and Joey are safer simply because they stay together.

The five men who form the clique at the Station cooperate in three arenas. They earn and spend money together; they collect and share resources; and they protect one another. And although Raheem's avowal that everyone at the Station is "one big family" is an exaggeration, it holds true for clique members. Their obligations to one another are clearly stronger than their obligations to the other men and women who live at the Station.

Cooperation helps them get by but not out. By sharing everything they have with one another, no one is ever able to accumulate enough money to get a place to live. Resource flows are too precarious and the amounts too small to be able to acquire a conventional dwelling. "Saving for a rainy day" is a luxury these men cannot afford. The reality, at least for the men in the clique, is that they are barely making enough to get by. The day's panhandling take, split at least five ways (and more when others come into the picture), is just enough to meet their daily needs. The men are running in place.[16] None falls behind, but none gets ahead either.

"Holding Out"

> We're not radicalists. I don't believe in society as it ex-
> ists, but I realize the reality that it does. Therefore, we
> pay attention to the rules. We pay attention to the rules,
> but we got our own rules. In other words, if someone
> steps into our world, they gotta follow the rules or they
> couldn't exist.
>
> *Gypsy*

Gypsy, a black man in his late fifties, has lived on the streets
longer than the five men in the clique. Gypsy prides himself on his street wisdom, his ability to recognize potential
enemies and allies. He spends his nights at the Station.
However, Gypsy—a wanderer, as his nickname suggests—
is not part of the clique. He is fiercely independent though
not a radical, as he indicates by saying, "I don't believe in
society as it exists, but I realize the reality that it does." Despite his beliefs, Gypsy understands the importance of rules
as well as the consequences of getting caught breaking
them.

There are a variety of rules for everyone who lives at the
Station. Some rules concern hospitality: Don't walk
around with your pants falling off, for this is disrespectful
to others; try, if you can, to provide a newspaper or crate
for someone to sit on when "conversating." Other rules
dictate conduct: Don't come onto the corner acting like a
"honcho," a big man, which would also be an expression
of disrespect; don't get into fights, which may bring un-
warranted attention from the cops. If you do get into a
fight with another resident, fight fair; and lastly, don't in-
terrupt when people are "conversating," which is considered rude. The most important rule, however, governs

sharing. And the strength of the obligation to share among clique members corresponds to the stringency of the consequences for those who "hold out" on one another.

The members of the clique, as discussed above, share resources with one another based on a principle of collective sharing. According to Sayjay, "If one person's got, the other person's got. It don't make no difference who's got the most. If I was to come up with a hundred dollars right now, I would give everyone ten dollars apiece, or maybe twenty dollars." Sayjay's statement exemplifies the clique's understanding, though often idealized and embellished, of the importance of sharing for survival. "What's mine is yours" is a prescription that governs life within the clique at the Station. The five men who are part of it harbor no notion of private or personal property.

"Holding out" to the men in the clique means withholding either possessions or information about possessions from others. It involves the expectation that others should tell the truth about their possession of resources. If good fortune befalls any one of the five, the others expect to be fully informed of it and to share equally. In practice, of course, good fortune is rare, and because the men spend so much of their money-making time together, issues of disclosure are not a daily concern. However, on the occasions when Sayjay stands in a police lineup or when Raheem helps out a hot-dog vendor, each returns to the clique and deposits the money in the "bank" for group use.

It is impossible, of course, to ascertain the level of compliance with the rule against "holding out." Surely there are infractions that go undiscovered. When a member of the clique is caught, however, conflict usually results. But unlike most arguments between clique members—over someone's drinking too much or interrupting private con-

versations—those concerning "holding out" may have serious consequences.

One day Ron discovered that Raheem had money that
he was not sharing with the group. Raheem had received
a check—the origins of which he would not disclose—for
three hundred dollars. Rather than sharing his good fortune with the clique, he spent the money on two prostitutes and a hotel room for the night. According to Ron,
"Raheem and I got into a fight. He was holding out on us.
He had some money and was holding out." When Ron
confronted Raheem, Raheem became angry and hit him.
Ron lost his footing and fell down. Raheem then took a
crate and crashed it into the side of Ron's face, leaving
Ron with a bloody left eye and a badly swollen jaw. A few
days later I asked Raheem about Ron's injured eye. Sayjay interrupted and grumbled: "What he [Ron] was doin'
was dead wrong. Rico and all of us saw the whole situation. Ron was dead wrong." When I tried to get more information about the fight, Sayjay quickly corrected me and
said, "We don't fight against each other. We get into arguments. We don't fight." Instead, Sayjay explained, Ron
and Raheem had "argued." By referring to the incident as
an argument, Sayjay and Raheem maintained a distinction
between clique members and other residents at the Station.
As they told it, Rico and George had had a "fight" whereas
Ron and Raheem had "argued." According to Sayjay, "All
we're gonna' do is smack you; we ain't gonna' beat you.
We are family." Ron, on the other hand, was more circumspect. To him the conflict with Raheem was a fight.
He dismissed Sayjay's claims that the clique was a family:
"They [Sayjay, Raheem, Rico, and Joey] are full of shit.
They're only interested in money. Since the Reagan era all
anybody was ever interested in was money. They are all

self-interested." He doesn't see them as friends either: "You don't fight with a friend. You may get angry but you don't fight. Friends would not let you fight."

This difference in perspective is explained by the fact that the burden of enforcing rules falls most often upon Ron. Members of the clique look to Ron for guidance and direction. "What do we do now?" they constantly ask him. Ron takes great pride in, as he puts it, "being an inspiration to other homeless people so that they can do something with their lives." He is seen by the men in the clique, as well as by many outsiders, as being very intelligent, resourceful, and different from the others because of his "gift," his singing.[17] On my visits to the Station, Ron seemed to know everybody there personally, including the police who patrolled the area. This combination of personal qualities and abundant "connections" makes Ron the uncontested leader of the group.

Though no one directly challenged Ron's position, clique members at times resented his attempts to exert authority and enforce its rules. After Ron challenged him for an instance of "holding out," Sayjay complained, "Ron is tryin' to take over everybody. He try to make everybody scared of him. Ron wants to be the boss. There's no boss. No bosses out here." Ron senses this resentment, "The men are envious, jealous of the way I carry myself. They are envious of the way I sing and dress." Usually, however, such feelings lie deep beneath the surface of group life within the clique. Raheem explains, "See, everybody down here [referring to the clique] on this corner, I don't know about anywhere else, but over here we look out for each other. Maybe once in a while we get into a little fight or something, but other than that, we look out for each other." Moses, an outsider who sleeps at a shelter but spends his days at the Station, concurs: "When friends fight, eventually it [the friendship] maintains. You just got to let them know that they're not going to take advantage."

Expressions of solidarity and selflessness coexist with instances of conflict and holding out. Sayjay, Raheem, Rico, and Joey embellish their relationships with one another, proclaiming themselves to be a family while occasionally acting in ways that appear purely self-interested. Ron, on the other hand, obeys and enforces the solidary obligations of the clique while refraining from ennobling them with the language of family. In his study of inner-city Chicago, sociologist Gerald Suttles found a similar antagonism. "Occasionally, reference is made to what people should be like, but a far more common concern is the actual character of people and one's own affiliation with them. There is, then, an explicit recognition of the ideal status of public morality and its undependability when applied to 'real people.'"[18] Sayjay, Raheem, Rico, and Joey may extol the "ideal status" of group solidarity within the clique, while its leader, Ron, is more acutely aware of what Suttles terms its "undependability."

Coupled with the strict rules within the clique is a less stringent but still important rule that applies to sharing beyond the clique. Above I described how clique members would not deny outsiders who asked to share resources. While nonmembers of the clique are not expected to offer the full extent of their resources to the others, they are expected to be honest when asked for help. As Sayjay explains, "If we give you, and you don't give us, then the next time we won't give you." Residents of the Station, therefore, risk being cut off from the sharing network if they respond to requests by saying they can't help when in fact they can. According to Gypsy, "There are things you do. I don't stash on him. I don't tell someone I have three thousand dollars and have nine thousand dollars in my pocket. Because if he finds out, you know."

Honesty is critical to maintaining sharing at the Station. Reputation for truth telling is very important. Gypsy explains:

> Your word on the street, you know, street people, is your bond and your bond is your life. If you're givin' somebody your word—I'm talkin' that I'm goin' to do this or I'm goin' to do such and such—and you don't keep it, you're fucked up. How can I be your friend if you give me your word and you don't keep it? If you got your word you got integrity, you got morals, you got ethics. You got to be more sincere with it, man. That's all you got. On the street it might rain on you, it might snow on you. You might be druggin' or somethin'. There are certain types of individuals we don't even like around us.[19]

According to Gypsy, one's "word" is a critical resource on the street. It assures others that you are being forthright and makes them more likely to share with you. A resident with a reputation for being dishonest finds it difficult to live in an environment in which survival depends upon sharing with others.

Rules regarding honesty at the Station do not differ from those among the housed. What is different among the homeless are the consequences of dishonesty. At the Station reputational stakes are high. Residents work hard to protect, maintain, and enhance their word. The profound concern with honesty starts at, but is not limited to, sharing. It permeates every aspect of homeless life at the Station. Consider a story related by Sayjay. A "girl," according to Sayjay, made a bargain with him. If Sayjay kept watch while she was having sex with one man, she would repay the favor by having sex with him:

> This guy is around the corner, him and his girl. It was late at night. I was sitting out there watching out for them while they were screwing. I had the girl's Walkman. I was just sittin' there listenin' to it waitin' for my turn. They get finished, she comes back, and it's supposed to be my turn now. She said that she didn't want to do it with me. I said, "Well, I could have took your Walkman and walked off with it." She said, "Well, you didn't take my Walkman and walk off with it. If you want it you can have it." She gave me the Walkman.

She had given him her word. As Sayjay says, "She gave me the Walkman because she didn't want to give me none."

Others damage their reputations by being labeled unreliable. Their word has little value. Crack users are ostracized at the Station: their relationship to the broad sharing network is marginal at best. According to Ron, he wrote his song "Get Off the Crack" because he "intended to offend people who smoke crack." Gypsy explains, "People who use crack can't keep their word because the drug is goin' to overwhelm their sense of responsibility and they don't respect themselves. They don't really know themselves." Crack, Sayjay claims, "makes you change. You start and you do [take] too much. You might get loud, you might get happy. You might get too happy and get into a man's face when he don't want you in his face. It's like that, you know. And that's when fights start." Like many others, the homeless view people who use crack as potentially violent and see them as threats to stability in an environment that, by definition, is unstable. Nonusers at the Station try to keep their distance. Gypsy explains, "Yeah, they can hang around, but they can't really get down. They can't really be a part."

Two distinct rules of honesty govern life at the Station. For the members of the clique, not "holding out" means volunteering information about resources. For those in the broader sharing network, one's word means telling the truth about one's ability to help when asked. Violations in the former case are resolved, with one notable exception, through ritualized conflicts and violations of the latter by avoidance or banishment. Banishment takes a bit of effort in an open and, for the homeless, attractive site like the Station, as the case of George illustrates. Sayjay explains, "He gets beat up all the time. What are we gonna do? Every time we beat him up he shut up for a while and then he comes back. He comes back like *Omen II*."[20] Toward the end of my stay, I noticed that George had indeed left the Station.

"They Are Associates"

> A person will see you all the time and they will see something that they like about the other person. It's the vibes. You have vibes. You have vibes before communication.
>
> *Sayjay*

Most of the time the men in the clique consider one another friends. For Sayjay, "a friend is someone you can carry on a conversation with," and Sayjay, Ron, Rico, Joey, and Raheem certainly spend great amounts of time "conversating." For the men in the clique, constant mutual companionship is an important reason they see one another as friends. The "vibes" that spark the friendships Sayjay enthusiastically speaks of represent his ideal of a magical first encounter with a stranger. But in reality friendship is the product of time and companionship.

The idea of friendship as companionship—continuously being together—complements an idea of friendship as profound mutual obligation. "We all love each other," claims Sayjay. "If one person goes, we all go," explains Raheem about the group's visiting hospital emergency rooms as a unit. Each member of the clique boasted a willingness to help others in times of need. And each, on various occasions, expressed concern for the particular circumstances of his friends. Ron pushes Rico to go to the hospital to attend to a cut on his neck; Sayjay pulls the sleeping Raheem out of the sun to prevent dehydration; Rico helps Raheem around in the mornings when his eye problem is at its worst; and all the men encourage Joey to stay "on the wagon" after his return from detox. All such acts were seen by clique members as acts of friendship, demonstrations of their commitment and sympathy for one another.

In terms of both companionship and mutual support, the men in the clique do not play favorites. I was unable to distinguish any pairs or subgrouping within the clique that lasted any longer than a few hours. None had a "best friend" in the group, though when I pressed each one to name the individual he felt closest to, Sayjay, Raheem, Joey, and Rico all named Ron. Sayjay refers to him as "my man." Raheem boasts that since the first night they met, he and Ron have "been together ever since." And Joey canvasses the Station in search of Ron, not the others, in his absence. Such a focus on Ron should not be interpreted to mean that he is everyone's closest friend but rather that as the clique's unofficial leader he is the individual most easily identified as a friend. In *Street Corner Society*, sociologist William Foote Whyte observed that Doc, the leader of a group of "cornerboys" (urban Italian American teenagers), faced a somewhat similar responsibility. According to Whyte, "The leader is the focal point for the organization of the group . . . the members do not feel that the group is gathered until the leader appears."[21] Sayjay, Raheem, Joey, and Rico all agree that "the party" begins when Ron is around.

Private relationships within the group are discouraged so as not to disrupt the group as a whole. I witnessed countless examples of one clique member's purposeful interruption of what appeared to be a private conversation between two other members. Such interruptions were at times resented, producing arguments between the men. Yet they were a constant occurrence; those whose conversations had been interrupted did not hesitate to do the same to others. I was often forced to "step off the corner" in order to talk with the men alone given that my attempts at privacy at the Station were always foiled.

Constant companionship is also constant surveillance. Much like adolescents in nightly telephone marathons, the men in the clique constantly check up on one another. The fear of private associations between clique members can be taken as evidence of distrust. Such distrust is most evident with respect to the issue of "holding out." The very existence of a rule against it, along with mechanisms for its enforcement, show that mutual support does not depend on friendship alone. Take, for example, the case of Raheem's check for three hundred dollars, discussed earlier. When Ron found out that Raheem had been holding out, a fight ensued between them. And although afterward the breach was repaired, it and other events like it have a lasting impact on the nature of trust between the men. This effect is most clearly expressed by the clique's leader, Ron. When in their company he refers to the men as friends; privately he is more cynical: "They are associates, you know, people you conversate with, socialize with. A friend is real, they are a part of you, they don't perpetrate things." In fact, researcher Carl Cohen, in a study of older homeless men, found a hierarchy of personal relations in which the term "associate" was used to denote relations that fell between casual acquaintanceship and friendship.[22] For Ron friends don't cheat or hold out on one another, as Raheem did. Unlike associates, they can be trusted more completely.

The difficulty the men in the clique have in living up to their own notion of friendship forces Ron off the corner to the company of Donald. Donald, the individual Ron identified as a friend, does not hang out at the Station. The two men meet regularly in the back room of a local coffee shop. Ron's friendship with Donald is contingent upon the latter's "being around"—that is, in close enough proximity to the Station so that Ron can find him yet somewhat distant from the corner and the clique of men.

Donald and Ron do not share food nor do they protect one another from the violence of street life. What they do is "conversate" without interruption. For Donald, the mutual dependence practiced by the clique corrupts the idea of friendship and holds his friend Ron back: "The guys are going nowhere. All they do is ask for money. They are only interested in what they can get. They'll drag you down. Every time I see them, all they want is money. Do they need the money, or do they just want the money?" The distinction between want and need is critical. Donald and Ron do help one another in times of need. But such instances are episodic and quite different from the daily and constant demands for mutual assistance that characterize life within the clique. When Ron asks for money, Donald literally asks if it is a want or a need, giving it only in the latter instance. And when it comes time for repayment, Donald asks Ron, "Is it enough to ask for it back?" Reciprocity is neither immediate nor expected. Such a distinction is inconceivable within the clique. Clique members, constantly under surveillance, do not need to keep mental accounts of who owes what to whom.

Ron and Donald's friendship is predicated on the fact that both trust one another to help in times of need and that such times are relatively infrequent. Constant need and dependency, as it is experienced in the clique, make matters more difficult. Were Ron to ask for money every day, Donald would be far less likely to accept his word that he needed it. What might be felt by Ron as need would appear to Donald as want, and resentment, suspicion, and distrust would follow.

Sayjay, Raheem, Joey, and Rico resent Ron's friendship with Donald and his more general practice of "stepping off the corner." While they accord him some privacy to write his songs, his absences often provoke distress. At times I would witness the men frantically searching for Ron, afraid that he might not return. As a leader, Ron is permitted to leave. Because he is key to everyone's welfare he has the power to claim some privacy. He is confident that the others will welcome him back upon return. The others rarely take such chances. Sayjay explains, "Somebody could conversate and say, 'Come on, let's go.' It could be like, 'Where you goin'?' And they just say, 'Come on.' Then you walk with them and you could go anywhere. They might have some static with somebody, and then all of the sudden you with them and you don't know nothin'." Sayjay's remark expresses the clique members' fear of being led astray. By keeping close tabs on one another, the men in the clique reduce their risk of entering into a potentially dangerous situation. Clique members, in particular Ron, would not lead them astray. Except for their group trips, therefore, the men in the clique are always at the Station and always together. Exceptions to this routine—Joey's trip to detox, Raheem's time with the prostitutes—are notable in the clique's reaction to the returning member. When Joey came back the men were elated. When Raheem came back they were suspicious. In contrast, Ron's absences, though they provoke concern, are routine.

The burdens of group life also deter close relationships between men and women. Beyond the difficulties posed by poverty and homelessness are the conflicting loyalties such relationships can engender. How different, after all, is the ideal of mutual support and protection between lovers from that between members of the clique? In word, if not always in deed, clique members feel obligated to take care of one another. That they do not develop such obligations to the women they sleep with is at least in part because such relationships would pose a serious challenge to group life.

The story of D.C. and Maria bears this out. D.C., a newcomer to the Station, was welcomed by the members of the clique. Strong, resourceful, and quick witted, he was seized upon by the others as a potential ally. He appeared eager to be a member of the clique, ingratiating himself with its five members. While still on the boundaries of clique membership, D.C. met Maria. "It was love at first sight. She came up to me. Everybody else was tryin' to talk to her, hit on her. She came up to me because I'm different from everybody else." Maria, a veteran of Station life, felt D.C. was different as well. "He's very different. He doesn't drink or use drugs. He's strong, he can protect me." D.C. boastfully interrupted, "Yeah, I can feed her and put clothing on her back." Maria would sit on D.C.'s lap when they hung out with the clique. They referred to one another as boyfriend and girlfriend. In the end, neither D.C.'s relationship with Maria nor his affiliation with the clique lasted. I returned to the Station after a few days' absence to find Maria gone and D.C. hanging out with a different group of men. Neither D.C. nor the members of the clique would explain what had happened.

Clique members on the street, like cliques of friends in high school, understand how girlfriends can weaken an individual's loyalty to the group. Sayjay, Raheem, Joey, Rico, and Ron were at first eager to welcome D.C. into the clique. D.C.'s relationship with Maria, however, undermined his chances. Although the men in the clique resent Ron's relationship with Donald, their resentment is nothing compared to what would result if any of them were to acquire a girlfriend. The principle of collective sharing could not accommodate the added needs of a man who had to "take care of" a woman. What is more, the question of divided loyalties that such a relationship would provoke would exacerbate the problem of distrust from which the clique already suffers.

CHAPTER TWO

"Kindness for Weakness": The Shanty

THE SHANTY, A BARRICADED MAKESHIFT COM-munity, rests upon a hill that is completely visible from the adjoining streets and nearby bridge across the East River. Fifteen makeshift dwellings stand in this formerly empty lot. These "huts," as they are called by the twenty to twenty-five residents, are made from a variety of discarded materials such as pieces of wood and boards, cardboard, mattresses, fabric, and plastic tarps. The materials are fastened with nails, twine, or fabric. Homemade and store-bought locks secure the huts as well as the residents' personal belongings. The huts are lighted and heated with electricity. Sammy, one of the residents, has tapped into a source of electricity by running a cable from a lamppost on the adjacent bridge into several huts.

Home Sweet Home

ACE: You won't mess it up, Gwen.
GWEN: Well, you invite me in, and the last thing I want to do is mess it up.
ACE: You can't make a mess. You can't make it any worse than it already is.

Visiting Ace at "home"

I had heard about the Shanty but was still taken aback when I saw it. At first I stood across the street and just looked in. I was hesitant to enter. It was like a fortress, a dilapidated one, in plain view of the street yet unmistakably set apart from it. Others walked by the gated compound as if nothing were out of the ordinary. They barely looked at the place; I was fixated. Eventually I worked up the courage to walk across the street and go inside. A man approached me. I prepared to tell him who I was when others emerged from their huts: mostly men, a few women. Susan was the first I ended up speaking to.

Susan, ashen, dark-haired, in her late twenties, bore some physical resemblance to me. She informed me immediately and confidently that she would tell me "anything" I wanted to know. We sat outside her hut, and I listened as she spoke easily of her two and a half years in the Shanty. She told me it was difficult for a woman in this place; for instance, there were plenty of places in the neighborhood for men to take showers but none for women. She asked me questions: What was my research about? What kind of book was I going to write. Mostly her concerns were personal: Did I have a boyfriend? Were we going to get married? Did I have a picture she could see? I showed her a picture of my boyfriend. She showed me a photo of hers. His name was John. He had been rushed to the hospital with acute AIDS over the summer. She despaired of spending the winter without him:

> This is my first winter alone. Every winter, I tell you, I never even used the heater. I even had two, three blankets, tops. I mean I've actually sweat at night. I never caught a cold the whole time I was on the street. This is my first winter alone. I don't know how

it's gonna be. This might be the first winter that I do catch a cold, pneumonia, who the fuck knows.

Susan showed me her hut. It was cramped, barely large enough to hold one person. "I'm tired of crawling in," she complained. Inside, her clothes were neatly folded into piles on the floor. Next to her bed—a mattress on the floor—were crackers, a jar of peanut butter, a few candles, and a small electric heater.

We went back outside and continued talking. She told me how she made it to the Shanty. As a teenager, she worked for a temporary agency, eventually landing a word-processing job at E. F. Hutton, a Wall Street brokerage firm. Her father died; Susan became hooked on heroin. As Susan tells it:

I started when I was eighteen or nineteen years old. I used to go with this guy, right. His friends came up with a get-rich-quick scheme with heroin. He was able to get heroin, and he wanted us to help him cut it and put it in bags and sell it for him, and we would make a lot of money. I started to sniff here and there; before you know it, three or four days, you get hooked on it. When you get hooked on heroin you get sick. You get physically addicted. You don't want to feel like that so you sniff some more and you feel better. Before you know it you get hooked on it.

Susan's addiction grew, eventually causing her to lose her job.

Susan admitted to her older brothers and sisters that she was a heroin addict and asked for their help. Without her mother's knowledge, they put her in a hospital. After her release, she went to live with her brother and his wife in Rhode Island, where he worked as a personnel director. Susan had hoped that he would help her find a job in his company and a place to live. Instead he told her, in Susan's words, that "I had to come back to the City and face my problems head on and be strong." Despite her protests that she wasn't ready, he insisted. "When I came home a month later, I got hooked on dope again," she said.

Susan again told her brothers and sisters that she was hooked. This time they refused further help, informing her she was on her own and had to leave home. According to Susan:

> My mother didn't really want to throw me out. Even when she did throw me out she was lettin' me stay with her, sneakin' me in. She even let my boyfriend, John, stay overnight. . . . One mornin' she had gotten sick. She was havin' a heart attack. If I wouldn't have been there, what would have happened? I called the ambulance. We took her to the hospital. And that's when my family found out that she was lettin' me stay there. They moved my mother out of that apartment. Some kind of senior citizen place outside the city. They would not give me her number. They would not tell me where she was. Three months later she died.
>
> Now if I would have been able to live with my mother until she died, I would have been able to keep the apartment 'cause my name was on the lease. I lived there twenty-six years. I wouldn't have been out on the streets. My mother always told me that I can't leave you anything, but at least I know you'll have a place to live. But then she listened to the family. They blamed her death on me. I didn't even go to her funeral. The day I

found out my mother died a friend told me in the street. When I called my sister she said that she didn't know if it was such a good idea to go to the funeral. They said it was my fault that my mother died. She probably died wondering where the fuck I was all that time.

After her mother died, Susan and her boyfriend, John, moved into the Shanty.

We talked some more about drugs. "Everybody up here uses drugs. There is no one up here that does not get high or drink," she said. She told me that she was currently enrolled in a methadone program and feared being dropped from it because of problems collecting the welfare that pays for the treatment. She seemed determined to beat her heroin addiction. Unfortunately, she told me, she had begun using cocaine, which, she claimed, was even worse: "I lost everything because of it [cocaine]. When I was using heroin it wasn't that bad. Once you start using cocaine, that's when you lose everything. Cocaine takes control."

At one point, Susan stopped midsentence to inquire, "When are you going to start asking me questions?" Susan, it turned out, had experience with interested outsiders. The Shanty was, by its very existence, a curiosity, the kind of place popular with local reporters who, as Susan explained, promise "to get the story straight," but instead

make up their own fuckin' version. You don't know how mad I was about that. The Post is always comin' up here and doin' some stories. My boyfriend agreed one time. And the guy that was doin' the story seemed really nice. Now, he [Susan's boyfriend] told him things about the lights and shit. Everything that we asked him not to write he wrote. Like with the electricity. I don't give a fuck but we're not supposed to have electricity. We're robbin' from the city. We could get into trouble. The cops, everybody knows about it, but they don't say nothin'. It's not something that you want published. That son of a bitch goes and he writes it, and like it was so disappointing because I thought he was really cool, you know. . . . Why even bother interviewing us if you're going to write what you want anyway?

Susan seemed angry, but her distrust of reporters did not extend to me. Perhaps it was because I was a woman, so close in age and in appearance to her. Perhaps it was because I showed her my boyfriend. Perhaps it was because I never asked her any questions.

Most of the huts are nicer than Susan's. Scattered about the lot, they vary in size and shape. One hut, constructed by one of the three Chinese residents, is built low to the ground and follows the sloping terrain of the hill. Featuring more than the usual one room, this was one of the first semipermanent Shanty dwellings. Others are taller, allowing occupants to stand. Sammy's "La Ponderosa," as a sign on the fence identifies it, is a fenced-in, ranchlike compound. Sammy borrowed the name from the Cartwright family ranch of the popular 1960s television series, *Bonanza*. Inside "La Ponderosa" are two huts that Sammy built. He and his girlfriend, Lisa, live in one; Sammy rents the other to Larry and his girlfriend, Elaine.

Though huts like Ace's, Louie's, Red's, Ollie's, and Juan's have one room and comfortably hold no more than one or two persons, they are quite literally packed with stuff. Inside the huts are beds, chests of drawers, chairs, tables, televisions, clothing, blankets, and electric heaters.

Some have stereos, hot plates, and toaster ovens. Acquisitions and donations are rarely thrown away. If they cannot fit inside the hut, they are stored directly outside for possible use in home improvements and repairs or for exchange. For example, an unwanted raincoat can be used as a tarp to cover cracks in the roof, or an unneeded piece of furniture can be dismantled and reused as a shelf or part of a wall.

The physical shape of the Shanty changes constantly and at times dramatically as residents remodel and refurbish their huts. Repairs occasioned by weather damage and fire, as well as ordinary wear and tear, are a daily necessity. Some residents, such as Sammy, Tito, Ace, and Red, continuously renovate their huts. Making them taller, extending a wall, or strengthening a roof expresses a sense of pride as well as permanence. Even while proclaiming that "this place is a dump," Ace went to great lengths to show me how he was going to put a shelf above the couch where I was seated. For Sammy, home improvements have proven profitable. When Sammy first moved in with Lisa, her hut was small and unsteady, barely large enough for one. According to Sammy:

> She used to have it just as a place to hang out. She used to live uptown and just stay down here because she didn't want to go uptown. She just wanted to hang out. She brought me here, and eventually I started to build it up. We were actually stayin' in another one which was low like hers. I built it in the middle of winter. I used to come out, warm up and do a little work, and then I built it up. And then I put in lights and things and heaters and then we moved in. I left the other one for a stockroom, you know, a closet to put clothes and things. And then this guy offered me

money and he lived there and then I built that one higher too.

Sammy also rents the space in front of his hut as storage space for fruit vendors and construction workers.

In addition to "hustles" such as Sammy's, the residents of the Shanty do a great many things to get by. As in the case of residents of the Station, welfare plays a minimal role in their lives. So difficult is negotiating the system that most forgo their entitlements. Susan explains:

> I don't get welfare. I just can't fuckin' do it. I hate those people in there. They make you fuckin' sit and sit and ask you questions that don't make any sense. It's none of their fuckin' business anyway. Either you're gonna give me the welfare or you're not. What is the point of all these fuckin' questions? You're homeless but you have to have an address. What kind of shit is that? Give me a break. They want you to get so fuckin' upset that you do get up and walk out. They test you. And if you do get up and walk out, that means you really don't want it.

Conventional labor plays a similar role here as well. Some of the men work as itinerant laborers. Employers often come to the Shanty in search of casual labor. One afternoon a man named Tony dropped by to ask if anyone was interested in helping him "haul loads of stuff" at seven the following morning. At forty dollars for a day's work, both Juan and Eddie happily volunteered. None of the residents, however, is consistently employed, though most are, at least some of the time, street merchants. They are veteran scavengers, spending much of their time rummaging through trash for items that can be sold on the street or traded with one another. Huts provide storage space for any number of things with potential commercial value. Ace spends his time "junkin'" items such as discarded radios, baby strollers, and furniture. Sammy strips copper from old plumbing and sells it. None of the residents panhandled or frequented soup kitchens.

Many of the women are prostitutes. Ginger, Lisa, Nina, and Elaine are "on the stroll" to earn money for themselves and their boyfriends. Richie explains how his girlfriend, Nina, first turned to prostitution:

> You see, I lost my job and we find ourselves doin' really bad. As a matter of fact what had happened was a guy pulled up and offered me a hundred dollars for Nina to take a ride with him. We were just walkin'. We were either on our way or comin' back from just copin' [getting some drugs], and we just hit the stroll [street or corner where prostitutes hang out] where I told you, Allen and Houston. As a matter of fact, we were waitin' for the light, I think. We were standin' and a guy pulled up in a brand new Mercedes, and the guy gets out and he comes over to me and offered me a hundred dollars for Nina to take a ride with him. I almost killed him. I almost murdered him. She asked me then, about a week later. We were broke, we were really broke. We were bad. . . . She said, "Richie, I know I could make a quick hundred. Let me stand out over here for a while. You watch me from across the street."

Jimmy's relationship with his girlfriend, Ginger, is similar. They live in the hut behind Ollie's. Both in their late

twenties, Jimmy is Chinese and Ginger is white. Both hustle. Ginger is a prostitute and, according to Susan—who
made sure that my tape recorder was turned off—Jimmy
has a "scam goin'" in Chinatown. As Susan tells it, Jimmy
and one of his "Chinese friends" go up to people—"mostly
Chinese people"—claiming to have lost their wallets and
asking for money in order to get home. If the person refuses, Jimmy and his associate "beat them up." Jimmy met
Ginger in the Shanty when she was living with Juan and
another friend. When their hut burned down, Ginger
moved in with Jimmy. They have been together ever
since. Jimmy is vague on exactly how he came to live with
Ginger; he claims he could have left the Shanty but stayed
on "only" because of her.

Although Susan recognizes the desperation of women
like Nina and Ginger, she blames Jimmy and Richie for
pushing them to prostitution. She has a hard time believing that a man can love a woman and allow her to do it:

> How can he be your boyfriend if your boyfriend lets
> you go and suck dick on the corner to get him high.
> And then you're gonna go to bed and kiss. And he's
> supposed to love you. Get the fuck out of here. I
> couldn't do it. Especially if I was doin' it for a man. If
> I had to do it for myself and it was something that I
> was able to do, fine, because I'm doin' it for me. For
> me to do it and bring the money back and give it to
> a man, fuck you. Take the guy Ginger lives with, this
> little skinny Chinese asshole. . . . He loves her, he
> loves her, he loves her. But yet they fight when she
> doesn't want to go out and make money. Come on,
> man. You're not supposed to let her go out and make
> money. You say no, bitch, stay home. You know he

will go out and make money. But they smoke crack and you always want more, and then he gets in an attitude and she don't want to fight with him, so she'll get up and go out and make money. And she got to go out and suck dick to make some money.

Prostitution is dangerous business. The women of the Shanty recognize the risks they take of being beaten by customers. Susan told me of a woman she met while Susan was in jail for shoplifting: "This girl had like stitches from her neck down to her groin because this man like sliced her. I would be scared gettin' into a car with somebody I didn't know. There are some sick men out there."

Ginger was once beaten so badly that she ended up in the hospital. "I got the shit beat out of me. He strangled me. I almost died. He was goin' around doin' it to all the young girls. He was a young kid, just lookin' for crack," she said.

In marked contrast to the violence that women fear "on the stroll" is the relative safety they and the others feel when inside the Shanty. I discovered no instances of violence within the Shanty, either in my personal experiences or in the recollection of residents. A broken-down but visible fence surrounds the Shanty and keeps most outsiders away. There is only one entrance. The single point of entry means that residents can watch who enters the Shanty more completely than at an open, boundaryless site like the Station. What's more, though residents may argue with one another, they stop short of physical violence. Susan explains:

As a matter of fact, I feel real safe up here. I feel more safe up here than anywhere else. The guys, they look out for me, they do. They make sure that if somebody was comin' to hurt me, and I called out, I'm pretty sure they would help me. I don't think they'd let anything happen to me. Like yesterday, I was havin' an argument with somebody and the person was tryin' to knock my place down. My friend Ed was here and he jumped up and stopped the bullshit, you know. It really made me feel good because I knew he would help me and wouldn't let anything happen to me. It was over something really stupid anyway.

I asked Susan what the argument was about. She replied, as though the answer were obvious, "Drugs."

Drugs, in fact, play a central role in the day-to-day life of the Shanty. Unlike the Station, where crack, cocaine, and heroin use are not tolerated by clique members, the Shanty is known even among many homeless people who live elsewhere as a haven for hard-core, seriously addicted drug users. The tragic quality of their lives is evident in the story of Ollie.

Ollie, thirty-four, is from Yemen and claims to hold a degree in business administration. More educated than the other residents, he shares a penchant for crack as well as gambling. He started a business in Coney Island, but it failed. He tried to peddle some of his merchandise on the street, but it was soon confiscated by the police because he lacked a peddler's license. Like the other residents of the Shanty, Ollie is thin. Of average height, he has a dark complexion and hair. His dress gives little hint of his origin. Only his practice of wrapping his head in a scarf in rain suggests his Middle Eastern origin.

Ollie desperately wants to stop smoking crack but feels it is impossible as long as he lives in the Shanty. Avoiding crack leaves more money for other things, Ollie notes, explaining that he is richer during periods of abstention. But these episodes are short lived, and Ollie eventually succumbs to temptation. As Ollie puts it: "Life is ridiculous. What in life is worse than this? If it were gonna get worse, than I would decide to die or go to jail. Either way, there is nothing worse than this."

Just as Ollie seems to move in and out of drug use, so too he claims to move in and out of the Shanty. He is always packing to leave for Washington, D.C., where he has a cousin. Yet I would see him on each of my visits to the Shanty. He wanted to ask his family for help, he explained, but felt ashamed to. The last time I saw Ollie, he was trying to sell a calculator and a leather bag so he would have enough money to buy some cocaine.

Many of the residents have addictions so severe that drug use is more about "staying straight"—that is, neutralizing the harsh and debilitating physical and psychological effects of withdrawal—than about getting any sort of pleasure. For them drugs are a way to stay well. Tito, for example, started using heroin in the 1950s. "You know that commercial that suggests no one wants to grow up to be heroin addict; it's true. No one wants to be a heroin addict," he says. He does not, he claims, get high anymore. Rather, he shoots up "to stay straight, so I don't get sick." Jimmy puts aside a few extra dollars each week, earmarking the sum for a fund he refers to as his "straight money." Red, Tito's immediate neighbor, spends most of his days—or at least the days he is strong enough to get out of bed—rummaging around the Shanty for things to sell so he, too, can "stay straight." His addiction has taken its toll. His long, vibrant red hair, coupled with a slow and deliberate gait, pale skin, and drawn face, make him appear very fragile and sickly, older than his forty-five years.

Exceptions to this pattern but no less tragic are Louie and Jim, men in their sixties who see themselves as "Bowery bums"—long-time alcoholics who have lived in and out of flophouses and now live in the Shanty. They do not use drugs, but they do drink. Jim and Louie have known each other for fifteen years. They spend the better part of each day together, drinking, reading the newspaper, and selling bottles and cans for change. As Louie puts it, "we bum around." Louie, like many of the residents, has tried to beat his crippling addiction. Susan expresses a frustration that might equally well be directed at herself: "He annoys me because he frustrates me sometimes 'cause I see him sit there and actually go through the withdrawal from the wine and be sick and say, 'Sue, I'm not gonna' drink no more' and all this, and a week later he'll go and get a fuckin' bottle and get trashed." Fierce addictions, whether to drugs or alcohol, shape the lives of Shanty residents. Though Ollie may claim that he would "rather eat than smoke [crack]," his life, as well as that of the others, is inescapably organized around the acquisition and use of heroin, crack, cocaine, or liquor. It is no wonder that he and the others remain in the Shanty where authorities and the outside world pretty much leave them alone.

Fences and Walls

> There are very few people that I let come into my house and get high. Smitty is one of them. There are maybe two other people that I do.
>
> *Susan*

The police, residents of the bordering neighborhood, and people traveling along the busy streets nearby are very aware of the Shanty and its inhabitants. There is a certain official and unofficial tolerance, a common understanding between the men and women who live in "huts" within the fence on the hill and the shopowners, commuters, and neighboring residents who share this bustling downtown area. Shanty dwellers have limited contact with, but are not significantly constrained by, outside authority. Sanitation workers collect their garbage; the fire department may be summoned when a trash-can fire gets out of control or a shack burns down; the police may come in response to a specific complaint. In one instance, a police officer requested that Shanty dwellers move their latrine so that his mother, living in a nearby apartment, would not see it from her window. As a general rule, provided they do not attract attention to themselves, they are left alone, more objects of curiosity than of efforts at control. Smitty describes one visit by the fire department: "They just wanted to look around at the houses so they can have something to talk about. They want to say to their wives that they saw a homeless guy. That they saw the homeless guys." Some city workers, in fact, altogether refuse to enter the Shanty. On the night that John, Susan's boyfriend, was taken to the hospital, paramedics refused to set foot inside the Shanty. Instead, a couple of police officers and residents were asked to carry him to the ambulance.

Residents appreciate the benign neglect of the authorities and work to preserve it by attempting to enforce a general prohibition on activities that might call attention to the Shanty. Sammy has a difficult time following such rules. On one particularly cold and windy day, he built a trash-can fire that provoked a nearby apartment dweller to call the fire and police departments. A frustrated Smitty complained to me, "Now didn't I tell him not to make that fire? You don't make a fire when the wind is blowing." A similar desire to avoid public notice prompts residents to refrain from voiding and fighting in locations visible to outsiders.

Residents also attempt to avoid trouble by refraining from selling drugs to outsiders within the Shanty. According to Susan:

> Nobody up here sells drugs. The only thing they do is come up here and get high. Nobody up here sells drugs. First off, we wouldn't allow it. Second of all, we couldn't because the cops know exactly what we do up here. If we were selling drugs up here you would see people constantly coming in and out of here to buy.

While drugs and money certainly change hands within huts among residents and a few regular visitors, Shanty dwellers do make a conscious effort to avoid allowing the place to become anything worthy of police intervention. On several occasions, I observed residents reprimand Ace for selling drugs to too many strangers.

Their precarious claim to their space on the hill makes Shanty dwellers keenly aware of outsiders who pass through the gate. Some are and remain strangers. Nearby high school students or construction workers on a work break come into the Shanty to get high. They become familiar faces, but that is all. They do not socialize with the homeless in the Shanty, nor do the residents attempt to strike up conversations with them. More friendly visitors are also commonplace. Some enter into business partnerships with residents, working with them selling furniture and clothing on the street. Roger, a young man in his twenties, "scraps"—that is, finds things to sell—with Ace. Smitty, a frequent visitor of Susan's, lives at the Bellevue Men's Shelter but hangs out in the Shanty. He met Susan selling cocaine. As he tells it, Susan was three dollars short, he gave her a break on the price, and the two became friends. Smitty often comes by in the morning to wake Susan up so she can get to her methadone program on time. As much time as he spends in the Shanty, he never stays overnight.

Some visitors do stay overnight. A friend's hut in the Shanty is welcome refuge for those either between or without housing—a situation common among the many associates of Shanty dwellers. On one occasion, a couple tried to extend their visit indefinitely. Louie, one of the first Shanty dwellers, let Nina and Richie stay overnight in his shack. One night turned into two and two into three, and eventually the situation seemed permanent. This put Louie in an awkward situation. He did not want to throw them out on the street, but he wanted his home back. Louie had a problem, according to Susan, on account of his "being too soft and having a heart that's too big." Eventually he simply tore his shack down. Smitty explains:

> Louie got mad and tore it down because the people took over his house. He was stayin' outdoors. I came by the other day and he was stayin' out in the rain. I told him to go in his house. Yeah, they took it over, a couple did, they just took his house. Louie just got so mad that he tore the whole thing down.

Sometimes the line between visitors and residents is quite blurred. Jenny often stays overnight at Juan's. According to

Juan, she stays weeknights with him. She has sex with him and supplies him with crack. On weekends her husband, who lives in a public shelter, also stays with them. In return for Juan's hospitality, Jenny's "old man" gives Juan twenty dollars each weekend.

Blurred though they may be, boundaries between residents and visitors, as well as between individual residents, are very important in the Shanty. Here there are two kinds of space. The hill itself is shared space, and within it there are various private spaces, the huts. In their shared space residents can, if they desire, cook and eat meals together, socialize, or even bury their pets in a small communal cemetary. In their private space, they can be alone, their activities invisible to others. Unlike the clique at the Station, Shanty dwellers enjoy their privacy. They need not "step off the corner" in order to secure a private moment. What's more, the privacy afforded by the huts is intrinsically connected with a strong and almost jealously guarded sense of private property. Susan explains:

> Oh, I love my privacy. I love bein' by myself. I can go into my house and close the door. If someone wants to come over, I can say no. Sometimes people are assholes and think that because I'm in the streets, and that this really isn't a house or an apartment, that they can walk in and take what they want. No, baby. This is my house and these are my clothes and whatever's in here is mine.

Juan concurs, "When someone's in their hut, it's private. What's in your pocket is yours and what's in my pocket is mine." Huts are seen as extensions of those who own them. They are respected accordingly.

As in a well-ordered suburb, then, Shanty residents acknowledge two sets of obligations. One is to maintain public or communal space; the other is to respect the point at which shared space ends and private space begins. Closable doors afford Shanty residents discretion and control. Each may choose who may enter and when. One does not enter another's hut in the Shanty without knocking or getting permission. Consider as evidence an instance when this second obligation was breached. Susan explains:

> I would never walk into somebody's house without knocking. If they weren't home, I wouldn't go in. For example, I have a wrench to open up the fire hydrant. A couple of times when I wasn't home Sammy would just go in and get it. Sammy has done that. It annoyed me a lot at first. I would never do that. I would never just go into anybody's house. I told him, but in one ear and out the other. He did it again. But he shouldn't and he knows he shouldn't. It doesn't seem to penetrate.

Susan asked her boyfriend, John, to threaten Sammy, to "convince him that he would be better off not doin' it again." The borrowing stopped. As a consequence of such occasional failures to respect private property, many residents put locks, both homemade and store-bought, on their huts. Sammy locks the gate surrounding La Ponderosa, as well as his and Lisa's hut. Louie, after rebuilding his hut, put a lock on the door. Curiously, Susan's hut remains unlocked.

For Susan and other Shanty dwellers, the huts provide basic amenities and opportunities not enjoyed by those at the Station. They can store and protect personal belongings without a fee. They can attend to at least some sanitary needs and change their clothes without having to find a public restroom. And they can—in a way impossible at the Station—relax by themselves, whether by watching TV, reading, or just resting and sleeping alone. "Anybody can do what they want in their own home," Sammy explains.

Huts are a social resource as well. Sexual relationships, so difficult to sustain at the Station, are facilitated by private space. Sammy and Lisa, Larry and Elaine, Ginger and Jimmy can live here as couples in separate huts. Close relationships between community members and visitors are also easier. A visitor need not pass muster with the entire group, nor socialize with it, as at the Station, but can maintain a relationship with one or two residents. As a consequence, the social world of the Shanty appears more layered and less dense than that in homeless sites where there is little distinction between public and private social space. With privacy and property comes as well the potential for hospitality. Residents of the Shanty clearly benefit from their ability to invite visitors into their homes. In the case of Susan and Smitty, such hospitality becomes part of an informal exchange. Smitty, it will be recalled, does not live at the Shanty. Susan, however, allows Smitty to use her hut when he visits. Smitty, in return, brings her the occasional stash of clothes.

Privacy also allows residents to do drugs alone. Consider the case of Juan and Ollie. Their huts are connecting. They often eat their meals together, and they often smoke crack together as well. One evening Ollie asked Juan if he had picked up his unemployment check. It was getting dark and Ollie wanted money for dinner. Juan told Ollie he had not received his check and that he would have to go back to the unemployment office the next day. Juan then quickly darted into his hut and closed the door. Ollie laughed, "He does this every time. He says he doesn't have money. I know he is smoking crack." Ollie walked over to Juan's hut and knocked several times on the door. Juan did not open the door. Ollie kept knocking. Several minutes later, Juan came out. Ollie laughed. He found Juan's failure to share with him funny. What would have been a serious breach of communal standards—"holding out"—at the Station was sufficiently commonplace to be humorous at the Shanty.

The ability to consume in private makes sharing entirely discretionary at the Shanty. Sometimes Juan shares his drugs with Ollie; sometimes he doesn't. What's more, the two can share with one another without necessarily including any of the other Shanty residents. Private spaces allow exchanges and relationships to occur outside public scrutiny. In the Station, the men have to "step off the corner" in order to engage in any private relationships. In the Shanty, they need merely go inside their huts. And once inside, unwanted requests by neighbors, specifically requests for drugs when they are not offered, can be avoided.

Using drugs in public is, in fact, somewhat taboo within the Shanty. Residents are expected to use drugs inside their huts. On no occasion did I witness any resident using drugs in public space. I was told that this was simply a matter of "etiquette." Richie explained that using drugs in front of a nonuser is disrespectful:

It's common knowledge in the drug culture. For me to just take my works out and shoot, I would feel uncomfortable in front of you. It's not right. If I was just to turn around and put a needle in my arm, it's disrespectful. You might not see it, but from our point of

view, it's disrespectful, very disrespectful. God forbid,
I could be an influence. I could cause you to do it.
You never know.

The proscription against public drug use, part of what
Richie called the "drug culture," is not specific to the
homeless. It displays the belief shared by many residents
that using drugs in the presence of a nonuser is "disrespectful" and may be unintentionally "influential." One
night I was at the Shanty later than usual. The door to
Ace's hut was open. I looked inside and witnessed a man
shooting heroin. It was the first time I had ever seen this,
and I stood transfixed, staring, fascinated by the blood in
the needle. The man looked up and saw me watching him.
He let out a piercing yell. Startled and embarrassed, I
walked away, angry at myself for having violated his privacy, for having not shown him the proper respect. Over
time, however, I came to learn that the proscription against
public drug use was about more than just respect. It was
also a matter of simple supply and demand. Unlike the
cheap beer and fast food that are the staples of group life at
the Station, there are never enough drugs to go around at
the Shanty. "Holding out"—at least when it comes to
drugs—is a virtual necessity.

"It's a Nice Little Community"

> Sometimes they share. It seems like they share drugs
> more than anything else. It depends on who it is. The
> majority of them . . . Louie, that brother shares with
> everybody. I share. Sue, she don't share, very seldom.
>
> *Ace*

In 1988, Ace's world crumbled:

> My oldest daughter was killed in a car accident when
> I was in Philadelphia. When I came back I lost my job
> here. I drove a truck for a Chinese plumbing supply.
> On Columbus Day I happened to call my wife and
> found out she wasn't there, that she had been dead
> and buried. She died of a brain tumor. Things just fell
> in all around me. I was on a suicide mission. I was
> doin' all kinds of shit, tryin' to get myself killed.

Ace lived in a single-room-occupancy hotel until he lost
his job, then squatted in an abandoned building until the
building was renovated, and then lived in a car until he became sick. Ace is HIV positive. After his release from the
hospital, the authorities insisted that he live in a public
shelter. His stay at the shelter was brief; as for many of the
homeless, shelter life proved unbearable. Ace eventually
made his way to the Shanty: "We work together and have
our ups and downs. Living up on this hill it's like a great
big family." Shabby clothes and a scar-torn face make Ace,
a man in his early forties, seem somehow more worn than
the others. In the Shanty Ace has finally escaped the physical rough and tumble of street life.

Ace's speaking of those he lives with as "a family" reflects a common situation: many of New York's homeless
live their lives in groups comprised of other homeless people. Like the men in the clique, few residents in the Shanty
were in contact with housed relatives; and among those
who were, visits "home" were rare. A mixture of banishment (recall Susan's siblings), shame (Ollie and his cousin
in Washington, for example), and pride keep them away.
Lisa, Sammy's white southern girlfriend, is not welcome

home because of her involvement with Sammy, who is Puerto Rican. Ace claims that he could go home if he wanted to: "I'm independent. I know I could go to my sisters, but I got to do it on my own. Livin' up under my family, I couldn't do it." Ginger carries her mother's phone number in her pocket but never calls. Shanty residents, like many homeless I met in other locations, live with a distinguishable "crowd" of regulars whom in good times they refer to as "family."

Like the men at the Station, many of the residents often eat together and talk about what is going on in and around the Shanty. Such groupings, however, are more informal than at the Station. That is, they tend to be based on who is around at a given time. One Sunday evening, for example, Ollie, Sammy, and Juan were standing around a barbecue made out of a small pail with a grill on top. Ollie was cooking fish and yams. The three men shared the meal, setting aside a portion for Red, who was not well. Attendance at such gatherings is hardly compulsory. Two Shanty residents, in fact, choose not to participate at all. Both Chinese, one built the first hut erected in the Shanty. He comes and goes through a concealed entrance in the back of the Shanty. The other lives in a hut in the middle of the Shanty. He is less reclusive than the former but still tends to keep to himself. Neither speaks English nor interacts regularly with the others.

As at the Station, the residents of the Shanty share crackers, doughnuts, cigarettes, and clothing. Susan keeps a supply of peanut butter and crackers in her hut. One Saturday morning while we were hanging out, Jimmy knocked on Susan's door asking for something to eat. Susan took out a package of crackers and gave it to him. I saw and heard of many other such acts. Sammy boasts, "I give [Susan] clothes all the time." Smitty and Louie also bring Susan clothes. Ginger gives her old clothes to Elaine and Lisa. Ace shares cigarettes with Ollie and Juan. At one level, material possessions seem to flow rather freely among and between members of the "family."

Underneath what may appear to be simple sharing is an abiding concern with reciprocity. Richie explains, "It's only because they know they're goin' to get it back. There's no giving out here."[1] Shanty residents, in fact, usually view their exchanges of goods as trading rather than sharing. That one must give as well as take is a pervasive norm in the Shanty. Reciprocity is often not immediate nor its terms explicitly specified. However, when one resident offers something to another, it is expected that at some point in the future the favor will be returned. There is no collective "bank," as at the Station, no common pool of resources. Rather, trading accounts are kept informally between pairs of individuals. Consider, for example, how Ace describes his relationship with Susan:

> Up here, it's good. It's a nice little community. We have our little scraps . . . and squabbles. Now I know that you know that Sue and I have our little problems. She ain't said hi and I ain't said hi for a while. But then, last night, I was talkin' to Sue from inside my house. She was in her house. She asked me if she could have a candle. I started laughin'. She asked me what was so funny and I told her that she can take and take and take, but in the end she will give.

Susan concurs, albeit more cynically, "People don't share. They're only your friends when you can give them something in return."

Residents barter rather than share, in part because they have at their disposal a variety of resources to draw upon. Of primary importance are their huts. Huts give residents a place to store exchangeable items as well as a place to barter one-on-one without feeling pressured to share with the other residents. At the Station, outsiders would often ask for a share of the clique's meal, in part because it was consumed in public. At the Shanty, residents can escape solicitation and scrutiny. To engage in a private transaction in the Station would require potential partners to "step off the corner," away from the group. In the Shanty, one merely closes his or her door. This facilitates private exchange relations and eliminates the pressure to share collectively, as in the Station. Sharing still occurs, but the dynamic is different. Ollie, Juan, and Sammy set aside a portion of their meal for Red out of kindness, not out of obligation. Had they not done so, none would have been sanctioned for "holding out."

Between neighbors, however, even what appears as casual sharing provokes concern over reciprocity. Complaints about different individuals taking more than they give are almost constant. Susan often complains that she gives more than she gets: "I don't mind givin' because I know we all need. But nobody ever comes here and says, 'Sue, you want this? You need this?' Now if I don't need it, I'll see if anybody else wants it. But it never works the same way with me, man. Never."

A poignant incident illustrates the delicate and often precarious balances that residents attempt to maintain between one another. It occurred that same Sunday night as Ollie was preparing the fish and yam dinner. A loud scream came from La Ponderosa, Sammy's ranch-like compound. Sammy came running out of his hut, his finger wrapped in a shirt and yelling that he had sliced open his finger and needed Louie, who had antiseptic spray. Louie brought Sammy the spray but told him that he needed it back immediately because one of his kittens had an infected paw. Sammy got angry. He started yelling and screaming that Louie cared more about the cats than about him. Louie shrugged his shoulders and left. Sammy was still furious. Ollie tried to calm him down, but instead he became the object of Sammy's rage. Ollie tried to ignore Sammy and just kept cooking the food. Sammy went back into his hut.

When the yams and fish were finally cooked, Ollie prepared a plate for Red and brought it to him in his hut. When Sammy returned, he saw that some of the food was missing and again started to yell and scream. Ollie told him that he gave some food to Red, which, to Ollie's and Juan's surprise, infuriated Sammy. Again Ollie tried to calm Sammy down, without success. Sammy threatened Ollie, telling him that he better leave or else he was going to "get the shit kicked out of him." Sammy then picked up a few of the remaining yams, leaving the remainder for Ollie and Juan, and angrily marched into his hut, warning Ollie that he had better get out of the Shanty.

After Ollie and Juan ate their meal, Ollie went to visit Sammy. He was gone for quite a while. When he came back, he pulled a vial of crack out of his pocket that Sammy had given him as a gesture of apology. Ollie chuckled, "They don't want me to leave; they want me to stay." The vial of crack had, in effect, been exchanged for Ollie's forgiveness. Sammy used it to make things right between them.

There is, it would seem, no limit to the ways and means of trading and exchange within the Shanty. Residents often help build and fix others' huts in return for food, drugs, or cash. Sammy has gone one step further, setting himself up as a landlord. He rents one of his two huts to Larry and his girlfriend, Elaine. "Five dollars a day," boasts Sammy. "Five dollars a day for two people ain't too expensive. I mean two people a day can find five dollars panhandling on the street."

Not everything is for sale, however. Some belongings do take on a sentimental quality for at least some Shanty residents. Ace, for example, treasures a small gold key:

> There's a golden rule about gifts. You treasure them. You don't give them away, you don't sell them. I have right here a little key, a skeleton key. A little kid handed it to me four years ago. And every time somebody see that and say, "What is that?" I say it's a key to the world. I wouldn't give it to anyone if it was given to me. I treasure it.

Ace feels this way despite the fact that the key is an object with clear economic value.

The key notwithstanding, the fact remains that at the Shanty, survival is about buying and selling. The neighbors at the Shanty not surprisingly express the small businessperson's classic belief in the importance of self-reliance. To hear them tell it, they "get by" by being wily entrepreneurs and smart traders and by working hard. They acknowledge little dependence on one another. From the outside, the situation appears quite different. Residents of the Shanty cooperate daily in the creation of a flexible and personalized market based on barter rather than cash. They depend on one another's flexibility and leniency in the creation of exchange value and in the granting of credit. Their small reserves of cash would bring much less outside

Shanty walls. Though they are loath to admit it, each needs this community to survive.

"Don't Be Greedy"

> Poor guy, right here, Juan. They take advantage of him. They should take advantage of somebody who can handle himself. Don't take advantage of somebody that don't know how to fight or nothin'. And they all pick on him and they don't give him nothin', they take everything.
>
> *Eddie*

Sammy moved into the Shanty with some prompting from his girlfriend, Lisa. Originally from Puerto Rico, he has lived in the Shanty for four years. Like Susan and many others in the Shanty, Sammy uses crack. He has no history of heroin use, however. As a result, his body, in particular his arms, do not display ready evidence of intravenous drug use. He looks healthy. He is slim, with shoulder-length hair, a mustache, quick eyes, and an engaging, almost salesmanlike smile. Sammy is the entrepreneur of the Shanty. Referred to sarcastically as the "landlord" because he makes money from renting his second hut, he is also the "Con Ed man." ("Con Ed" is short for Consolidated Edison, the electric utility that serves the island of Manhattan.) Sammy has commandeered a supply of electricity by running a six-hundred-foot cable from a lamppost on the adjacent bridge into the Shanty and separate wires into several huts: "Nobody had lights here. I put the lights on. Shit, there are so many poles, but nobody knows how to do this. So I put the lights on." Sammy makes a profit by charging each resident for the initial hook-up. Both Ollie and Juan, for example, paid fifteen dollars for Sammy to hook up their electricity. And although Richie believes that such a practice is "vile," most of the residents, with few exceptions, pay for this service. Ace, however, refuses: "It's his con to get over. You get someone that is fool enough to pay, then do it. Me, I do without. I live by candlelight. I don't know why he charges them for somethin' that is free that he hooked up."

Why does Sammy charge the residents? And why doesn't he charge more? The answer lies in Sammy's philosophy: "They take kindness for weakness. They know you kind then they think you're weak. They use you. I don't let them do it no more. They know better, they know my temper." If Sammy gave all the residents the electricity for free, they would take his kindness for weakness and take advantage of him. If, however, he did not give them any electricity at all, or charged them too high a price, he would risk antagonism against him. His solution, to charge residents for their initial hook-up rather than for monthly usage, is, he thinks, a fair one. As he sees it, he is being kind without being weak. He claims he could make a lot more money than he does.

Concern about the relationship between kindness and weakness is felt by many Shanty residents. True believers in a property-centered self-reliance, they attribute their survival to their skill as traders rather than to the kindness of others. What's more, because they are constantly trading they cannot afford to have others perceive them as too kind. Kind traders, after all, do not get the best price for what they have to sell. They are seen as weak. "When he ain't got no money, nobody knows him," Eddie says of Juan, who is considered by others in the Shanty to be weak.

A particular conflict between Susan and Ginger over a bottle of perfume bears this out. On my second visit to the Shanty, I brought Susan two large bags of women's clothing and a variety of other items. The bags had been given to me by a friend who felt I "would know what to do with them." Susan immediately walked over to Ginger's hut and told her that there might be some "stuff" in the bags that she could wear. Ginger came over, and the two of them started rummaging through the bags with relish. Susan paused and asked if I had looked through the bags and taken whatever items I wanted. I told her I had. Susan smiled. She was relieved that, as she put it, I was "not a snob." Susan kept most of the T-shirts, shorts, and sweaters but gave two fancy dresses to Ginger. "It aggravates me because I can't use them," lamented Susan. "I have no occasion. It kills me to give them away. I love things like that, they're so sexy. But I don't got no use for it." There was, however, a small sample bottle of perfume—Opium—that Susan excitedly pulled from the bag. She held up the perfume to Ginger and said, "This is my favorite perfume, and you can't have it. No way. Sorry, Charlie."

The next time I saw Susan she told me that the envelope containing the perfume was gone. According to Susan:

> When I found that little envelope and the damn perfume was missing out of it I knew right away it had to be Ginger. Anyway, I was just so pissed off because I had given her these two fuckin' dresses. Those dresses were dynamite. If it had been the other way around she would have charged me. I'm not bullshitting. She would have charged me because she's a greedy bitch. And she just took the perfume and she did it sneaky. You don't want to be sneaky. Don't

fuckin' do that shit. I'm givin' you the damn shit anyway. Don't try to be sneaky on me.

Perfume, a luxury item even for those in more stable situations, has value for Susan both in its own right and for its
worth in exchange. When she discovered that the perfume
was gone, she was angry. She blamed herself for letting
Ginger think she could get away with the theft. As she explained to me, her "kindness was taken for weakness."

Though they may disparage kindness as a value, trading
in the Shanty is still significantly constrained by normative
considerations. At the Station, one's word is a means by
which others assess your worthiness as a sharing partner. If
you are not credible you will not be honest in sharing. At
the Shanty, where privacy allows some lack of disclosure,
and where boundaries between public and private belongings are both clear and jealously guarded, one's integrity is
assessed not in terms of one's openness to sharing but rather
in terms of one's fairness as a trader. Put rather simply, the
rule that governs social life at the Shanty is that it is all right
to be self-interested but not greedy. As Ollie explains, "It's
wrong to like money more than friendship."

When individuals at the Shanty trade, they expect that
their fellow residents will not take advantage of them. This
is not a matter of being kind in exchanges, which could be
perceived as being weak, but rather exchanging in such a
way that one party does not feel disadvantaged with respect
to the other. This is critical where both the flow and sub-
jective value of resources is uncertain. According to Ollie:
"We are all in the same boat. We are all homeless and we
should not take advantage of homeless people." The goal
is to drive not the hardest bargain but a fair bargain, one
that will facilitate further exchanges.

The extent to which residents of the Shanty avoid greediness is seen in their treatment of the one resident who frequently breaks the rules. Sammy, the entrepreneur of the Shanty, is often resented by the other residents:

EDDIE: He doesn't control a mother fuckin' thing up here. I can go and pull that wire out and he can't say a God damn word. He thinks he's like Don Juan and shit.

RICHIE: He does that with people he can get over with. He does that control with the electricity with the people that he can get away with it. He wouldn't charge Eddie. He wouldn't dare try it with him.

EDDIE: There are a few people he wouldn't try it with. He does it with people he can take advantage of.

RICHIE: He takes advantage of certain people. Ollie. Lou. Susan. The people that he can get away with it. He wouldn't try it with him.

Sammy is resented by Richie and Eddie because he presses his advantage in exchange in a manner that translates into control over others. Richie and Eddie object to Sammy's power over others in the Shanty. They claim Sammy does not wield power over them, although they too need electricity. His relative wealth is not the issue; power and the arbitrariness of power that comes from wealth is.

An incident that occurred during my time at the Shanty changed these circumstances. Sammy, it will be recalled, makes a profit by charging each resident an initial fee for hooking up their electricity. Several of the residents paid fifteen dollars for Sammy to do so. However, one night Sammy cut off all the electrical connections except that serving his hut. According to Sammy, he did this because there was a power overload. Too many people, Sammy claimed, were using heaters. Susan offers a different explanation:

> He just came home the other night and unplugged mine. He told me he unplugged it by mistake. He plugged it back in after I went bangin' on his door. And then, that night, out of the clear blue sky, everybody's went out. Now he said the wires shorted because there was too much power and everybody's plugged in their heaters. First off, no one had their heaters plugged in yet. Now he says he's not goin' to fix it again. Sammy's our Con Ed man. Sometimes he gets into one of his moods. When he doesn't think we should have electricity, we don't have it. I don't know why, he's just a jerk.

But according to Ollie, Sammy turned the electricity off because he is greedy: "Sammy likes money more than friendship. Sammy is greedy. Sammy takes advantage of homeless people. It's ridiculous because we're all in the same situation. Sammy's tryin' to make money off of people who don't have any."

I learned from Jimmy, one of the residents, that such "power outages" were common and deliberate and that after each, Sammy would charge another fifteen-dollar fee to reconnect a hut. This time, however, he had gone too far. Red spliced his own line into the power source, taking control over access to electricity from Sammy. Tito, his immediate neighbor, then hooked into Red's connection and began charging a few of the residents ten dollars, rather than fifteen, for electricity. He refused, however, to provide any power to Sammy. Ace, who begrudgingly purchased electricity from Tito, allowed Sammy to cut into his line, but when the others found out, both men were cut off and were without power.

The incident suggests that at the Shanty, violence is not required to enforce the rules, as at the Station. I never witnessed nor heard of violence between Shanty dwellers. Rather, residents were constantly "not talking to" one another in response to a perceived injustice. Ace and Susan, Susan and Ginger, Sammy and Ollie all went through periods when they would simply ignore one another and exchange nothing. Such sanctions were not available at the Station, where residents did not have the option of forgoing potential resources. In the Shanty, where exchanges are bilateral, problems with one partner do not translate into problems with the group. Sanctioning one person, then, is less consequential and disputes are more easily remedied.

The sanctioning of Sammy demonstrates the way in which expectations of fairness operate within the Shanty. His attempt to extract more money from his customers provoked their outrage to the point where they could be both unified and resolved to do something about it. What's more, their action represents a limit on the idea of private property in the Shanty. Before the incident, access to the power source was commonly understood as belonging to Sammy. Sammy's right in property was thus effectively seized by Tito in an action positively sanctioned by the community in response to his unfair and greedy practices.

Sammy's power, like Ron's, is the object of resentment by others. The reason—at least as residents of the two locations explain it—is different, however. Ron is resented because he enforces the rules, whereas Sammy is resented because he breaks them. And while feelings toward Ron tend to vary considerably according to circumstance, the enmity toward Sammy is constant, leading one to question why Sammy is allowed to stay at all. His status as a bad neighbor and an unfair trader is recognized by all, and the potential to gang up on him and force him out clearly exists. The answer lies in Sammy's particular talents for making money. Clearly the wealthiest individual in the Shanty, Sammy is, despite his character, a source of resources and wealth for the community as a whole. To throw him out would be to make the entire Shanty a bit poorer and is thus a luxury these people simply cannot afford.

"I Would Rather Have Friends Than Drugs"

> They will be your best fuckin' friends. Are you kidding me? They will do anything you want. If you asked them to wipe your ass when you take a shit they would do it. "I would do dis, dat, the other thing, everything and anything. Just give me drugs."
>
> *Susan*

The Shanty is rich in one-on-one relationships as well as nuanced distinctions among neighbors, friends, good friends, and lovers. Between different pairs of individuals are different and distinctive relationships, each carrying specific expectations and levels of responsibility. Unlike at the Station, where Raheem and Sayjay have identical expectations of Joey, Susan has very different expectations of Ace and Sammy. Relationships at the Shanty, unlike in any of the other sites I visited, are truly private. The privacy of the huts and the ability to escape the scrutiny of others enables residents of the Shanty to develop and cultivate the

mutual understandings required for one-on-one relationships.

At the Shanty the residents are all neighbors but they are
not all friends. As Ollie evenhandedly explains, "Some
people, they are very friendly. Some of them are your
friends [only] when you got money." For Ollie, there at
least two kinds of friends, the "very friendly" or true
friends who are there all the time, and others who are his
friends when he has something to offer them. More is expected of one type of friend than another. Susan was not
hurt when Sammy crossed her, that is, when he turned off
the electricity. She attributed it to his being "a jerk." She
was hurt, however, when Ace, as she tells it, put drugs
ahead of friendship:

> When a drug user needs their drugs they will go to
> the fullest extremes. They would steal from their own
> mother, so what makes you think that they wouldn't
> steal from you? . . . I thought Ace was a really good
> friend, and I found out otherwise and it really hurt
> me. It hurt me so bad 'cause I would rather have
> friends than drugs.

Sammy can make Susan angry, but he can't hurt her the
way Ace did. Ollie recognizes that Sammy "[likes] money
more than friendship." They still smoke crack together.
They still live next to one another. And most of the time
they still get along.

Friends at the Shanty expect more from one another
than they do from simple neighbors. Sacrifice, commitment, and general concern is expected from a friend.
Smitty, for example, tirelessly nags Susan to get tested for
AIDS. Red gives Richie a few magazines—which he usu-

ally sells on the street—to bring to his girlfriend, Nina, in jail. Ollie frets about Juan's well-being: "Juan's smoking crack too much. He's killing himself and he needs some help. He's my partner." For Ollie, Juan is not simply the man who lives next door; they are partners. Partners, he explained, are "friends."

Shanty residents are at times quite idealistic about the potential and possibility of friendship. Susan explains:

> A friend is somebody that's there when you need them. They're not just bein' a friend because they want somethin' from you. They're there to help you, not only help you, because you're in the same situation, but to be able to trust and talk to. And if I don't have it and you do, you give me. I mean to be able to share and help each other. Through anything and not just for drugs and shit. I mean, fuck the drugs. The drugs shouldn't have anything to do with it. That's what I consider a friend. Not somebody that I wouldn't be able to let stay in my house because they would take it. I want them to be able to ask me and know that they can have it.[2]

For Susan, trust between friends ought to be unequivocal. Friends, she explained to me, would not take kindness for weakness. But when she is in a cynical mood, Susan discounts even the possibility of such friendship. "Friends make promises they don't live up to. People talk a lot when they do drugs. Drugs have a good way of talking."

This contradiction is well explained by the particular circumstances of life in the Shanty. Like people in more stable environments, homeless residents of the Shanty expect help from their friends in times of need. Unlike in stable environments, however, need is almost constant, particularly among those maintaining an expensive drug addiction. Such constant needs and constant demands place strains on the bonds of friendship and can lead to conflict. People on drugs often sacrifice friends—even parents—for drugs. Tito explains, "It's cutthroat out here; there are no friends. A friend is a dollar in your pocket."

A fight with Ace during my time at the Shanty left Susan particularly disillusioned:

Ace and I got into a fight over drugs. I always give and nobody gives me nothin'. I always go and get. He never goes and buys anything and I'm always givin' him and I don't want to anymore. I feel really upset about it. It [the friendship] was really stupid and I was really hurt by it because I thought we were good friends. I thought that's what it was. I was really naive. I didn't even know that it was just for drugs. I always seem to get stuck by it. Either you're gonna have a really true friend that's gonna be there with the drugs or without the drugs. But most of the time they'll let you think that they're gonna be your friend but they never are. If you don't have it [drugs], then you're not there. I'm not like that. I'll be your friend through thick and thin. And I'd like you to be the same way with me. And don't let me think that you are [my friend] and when I don't have it [drugs] you don't want to know me. That shit really hurt me. I mean I was cryin'; I really felt bad. But you live and learn, right. Fuck it, you can fool me once but you're not gonna fool me twice. I won't give Ace the time of day no more. But I don't want it to be like that. I mean we all live up here, we should help each other. But it can't be like that. I can't believe that I was that naive. I mean I've been on the street a long time. I think I should know better. He actually fooled me into thinkin' that he was a real friend. He turned out not to be.

Ace expressed a similar dissatisfaction:

> I just learned not to get too friendly with anybody because they take kindness for weakness. Like when you use drugs and they know you got drugs and you're their best friend in the whole world. When you don't have it, you can go fuck yourself. I found that out. I think that's more important. Fuck the drugs. We're all friends but we're all homeless and we're all in the street. We should all be helping each other.

Viewed side by side, Ace's and Susan's explanations of their dispute are strikingly similar. The fact that each of these friends relies on the other so extensively to support their crippling drug addictions leads each to suspect the motives of the other. Friends who help one another can, in times of conflict, come to see such help as the sole basis for friendship. Susan gives Ace drugs and eventually suspects that the drugs are the reason that Ace is her friend. Feelings of kindness toward a friend are thus called into question by the fear that one is being taken advantage of.

Not all misunderstandings between friends lead to such consequential conflict. One day Ace saw an unattached jacket inside the Shanty. Thinking that it did not belong to anyone, he took it to a nearby street corner and sold it. Later that day Red asked Ace if he had seen the jacket. Ace grew upset at the realization that he sold his friend's jacket. He told Red what he had done and offered to give him some money when he had it. (He had already spent the money earned from the jacket on drugs.) Red told him not to worry about it, trusting that Ace had, in fact, committed an innocent mistake and had not intentionally taken his jacket.

That this incident did not provoke conflict testifies to a greater trust between Red and Ace than between Ace and Susan. Unlike Susan, Red was Ace's friend before they came to the Shanty. Such prior knowledge, important in leading some people to the Shanty, also contributes to bolstering trust between them. Ace explains:

> There are only one or two people I can trust, and one of them is Red and the other is my play brother, Larry, the one that lives inside the compound with Sammy. I just call him my brother. Me and him knew each other for quite a few years. We somewhat look alike, so some thought we were brothers. And Red— well, Red I've known for about ten years. I met Red in Philadelphia years ago. I did a job. When I came up here Red was already here. We hadn't seen each other in about seven years. I walked up here and I kept hearing somebody say Red. And I say he can't be talkin' about Red. I happened to be lookin' out and seen him a block away. I know the walk. I know that walk. That's the strange thing about me is that I can tell a person a block away by the way they walk.

Having known each other in better circumstances—that is, having come to trust one another before reliance on this trust became an everyday fact of life—Ace and Red can make allowances for temporary breaches that are the product of harsh circumstances.

Nowhere is the process of making allowances more visible than in the long-term monogamous love relationships that several Shanty residents enjoy. Love is an important part of life in the Shanty. According to Richie:

> Let me tell you, most of us, regardless of what people might think and say, most of us that might have a woman it's all we want. We don't look for anyone else. We really don't.
>
> Like I said, you got one woman, that's all you want. I'm happy just to take care of my woman. I'm satisfied with her. I happen to love my girl. Really, I know it sounds corny, but that's the truth. I was married for ten years, but I finally found the right woman. As a matter of fact, we're gonna be married soon.

Declarations of love, stories of finding the "right" man or woman, are made frequently by couples like Susan and John, Sammy and Lisa, Jimmy and Ginger, and Richie and Nina. Lovers at the Shanty stay together: each relationship has been going on for several years.

The second time we got together, Susan told me more about her relationship with John. Her story conveyed on one hand her love and devotion to him and on the other her anger at him for being gone. To quote Susan at length:

> I thought I found the right guy, but I don't know if he's alive or dead right now. The last time I saw him I had to call the ambulance for him. It looked like he was on a death mission, you know. He had just given up. He had double pneumonia, and he wouldn't go to the hospital. He looked like a skeleton when he left here.

Anyway, he had gotten an abscess on his arm. You know what an abscess is? You get it when you shoot up. And he cut it open himself, and it got infected to the point where it had maggots in it. You couldn't go within three feet of the hut, the odor was so bad. Now that's my old man, five years. Now how can I say I won't sleep with him because he stank, you know. The last two days when he was here is when it really did stink. Anyway, October second would make five years.

I miss him with all my heart, and I love him like you wouldn't believe. But it's not the same love that we used to have. Like he showed me what love was. I thought I loved someone before, but it wasn't. Like when I first met him we fell in love. When I first met him as soon as I looked at him, I knew something was there. And he tells me he felt the same.

He lived with me and my mother. We lived together four months before we ever went to bed or anything. We fell in love before we got into a relationship. He was my best friend. I used to confide in him in everything. And when I finally did go to bed with him and everything, it was really great. I will never forget that. It was so special. We used drugs, but the drugs weren't the most important thing. I was able to talk to him about everything. He was my best friend. I mean he was my best friend I ever had.

I hope to God he's not dead. But God forbid if he is, I don't know. If he isn't at this point, I let him down so bad. I just neglected him. I never went to visit him [in the hospital]. When he went away in the ambulance, that was it. Why didn't I go visit him? Why did I do that? I don't even know. Like I just couldn't look at him the way he was. I cried in bed and asked him why he was lettin' himself die. It was like so weird. He kept sayin', are you gonna' be all right if I left? He was so worried about me, and I just let him down. The hospital is in walking distance. But it is just somethin' that I can't even explain.

He's the only person I have. It was just me and him, together, through everything. A lot of times I feel he let me down because he was the man and he wasn't doing anything to help me. I mean he used to sit on his ass, and I used to go out and make money and bring back the drugs.

We were both using drugs when we first met. But like I said, the drugs weren't important. It was being together and doing things, that's what was important. You know, when we became homeless the drugs was the only thing we really had in common after a while. He just became so dependent on me, and I let him, which was stupid. I shouldn't have let him become so dependent, fully dependent on me. I would go and get up and get stuff for him. And he was very sneaky. If he had gotten some [dope] he would do it someplace else and not give me. And he thought I didn't know, and I did know. And why I would stay with him?

Everybody would tell me I was crazy because he was using me and shit. But he was the only person I had. I was afraid. But since he's been gone, I found out that I can survive by myself. But even if he did come back, I don't think that I would even want to be with him. I've gotten used to being on my own, and I know I can make it.

The love was there; it will always be there. If it

could ever be the way it was? I don't know. But as for the way it was before he left, I don't want, I don't need that shit.

Susan spoke of John at times as if he were alive and at others as if he were dead. She seemed to shift between expressing, on one hand, an abiding belief in love, and on the other an awareness that such love was not good for her. She commented that "even if he did come back, I don't think that I would even want to be with him." Later, however, she asked me a favor:

If I gave you his name and everything, would you like call the hospital and find out if you can find out anything about him. Because I'm at the point where I'm afraid to call because I don't know if I really want to know. But if you did it and told me, I wouldn't mind, you know. Whenever you get a chance.

On subsequent visits we didn't speak of John, but I could tell she continued to long for him. She would, as we spoke, scribble their names everywhere: on pieces of paper, on the walls of her hut or her water jug, and into the dirt beneath her feet.

John, I had learned from others at the Shanty, had AIDS. Late during my time there, his former neighbors checked on his condition and learned that he was dead. The news led to a great change in Susan's life. For four months she had waited with the hope, however faint and ill founded, that he would return. Upon learning of his death, Susan moved out of the Shanty and went to live with a couple she had met in her methadone program. They kicked her out when, after having given her "a lousy forty dollars" to get a couple of bags of cocaine, she produced neither the money nor the drugs. She returned to the Shanty and stayed briefly with Jimmy, who kicked her out when she took twenty dollars, his "straight money." She then stayed with Ollie for one night. According to Ollie, it was terrifying. In her attempts to "get high," she desperately and unsuccessfully poked her arms and legs looking for a vein into which to inject cocaine. Blood—"her contaminated blood," as he put it—spurted everywhere because she could not find a fresh vein. He too asked Susan to leave. According to Jimmy, "Susan is screwing everybody. Soon she will piss everybody off." Ace finally took her in. According to Tito, "Ace always wanted her and now he can have her. They deserve each other."

The news of John's death laid bare a stark reality many in the Shanty found difficult to face. Although Jimmy, Tito, Ollie, and Eddie privately understood that prolonged substance abuse, prostitution, illness, and poverty could and probably would deliver them to a similar end, they chose to condemn Susan publicly for "letting John die," maintaining that it was somehow her fault that he died. Tito told me that Susan was the most "cold-hearted" woman he had ever met. She could have helped John, he claimed, "but didn't. . . . Maggots infected his arm, she didn't do anything." Eddie spoke of the times that John would wander out of his hut at four o'clock in the morning, delirious and wearing a cloth to cover his face. He would lie in the hut all day and only come out late at night to talk to Louie, who would be up drinking. "Susan would give him a shot of coke to get him straight, but she never took him to the hospital," complained Eddie. In John's death these men quite simply saw their own. Lashing out against Susan allowed them to ignore this reality. Even the usually cynical Tito declared, "I would have carried my brother out, and he would do the same for me. She let him die."

Similar hard times fell upon Jimmy and Ginger during my time at the Shanty. When I last spoke to Jimmy, Ginger had been missing for over a month. At first, the residents thought that she was in jail. Jimmy found out, however, that she had not been arrested. I asked if Ginger might be dead. Jimmy just stared into the trash-can fire. He said that someone had told him that he saw her in jail, but that some of the residents in the Shanty told him that she was dead. He told me that he once had Ginger's mother's phone number but that he lost it. I asked him why he didn't call information. He shrugged his shoulders and said that he was just going to wait.

Jimmy stayed in the Shanty. A month later, Ginger was still missing and Jimmy was living alone, still waiting for her to come back. He said that he would not leave until he knew for sure that she was dead. According to Ace, "Jimmy misses her, he really misses her. He admitted it yesterday. Me and Jimmy and Eddie were standin' out here talkin'. He said he was goin' to go to the Second Avenue precinct to check on her again. He yelled, 'God dammit I miss her, so what, I miss her.'" Like Susan, Jimmy refuses to seek final confirmation of Ginger's death. Though she is in fact gone, the lack of conclusive information permits him to harbor at least some hope of her return.

Sammy and Lisa have been together for over four years. Though Lisa could move in with her family, she chooses to stay in the Shanty with Sammy. According to Richie:

Lisa's originally from West Virginia or something. Her parents once told her to come home. She was

telling me this story. She didn't want to leave him
[Sammy]. This was a couple of years ago. Her mother
wanted her to come home and told her don't worry,
we'll help you out, just don't bring him. I don't know
if she sent a picture of him or she described him or
anything, but the mother sounded prejudiced. She
said don't bring that Puerto Rican. Anyway, I remember she went home for a week or two and then
came back. She went home to like pave the way, so
to speak, and to try and like smooth things and to get
her mother to like try and accept him. She was goin'
to bring him. But evidently I guess she couldn't get
through to her mother because she came back. Like
she went down and came back, and they were supposed to pack up and go and they never left, so evidently the mother does not want anything to do with
her. Apparently her mother said you come alone or
you don't come at all. She won't leave him. But this
was then. It becomes like a trap. You may be in love
with the person and you won't leave them at that particular time, and as time goes on it becomes impossible to leave. And you may not be in love anymore.

Sammy and Lisa support one another. Sammy has his many
businesses, and Lisa is a prostitute. However, some of the
residents feel that Lisa gives more than she gets. In fact,
many of the residents were angered that Lisa continued to
work while she was pregnant with Sammy's baby. According to Richie:

It's bad enough havin' your woman be out on the
stroll but you got no choice in the matter because
you're sick and your addiction takes over. As far as her

being pregnant, well, my morals and my values have like gone down the drain 'cause of my addiction, but there are still a few things that I hold true. I couldn't allow my woman to be out there pregnant. And it's like not a question that he don't know. He know, he keeps track of her. He spies on her all the time. He'll stand like half a block away and he'll watch her every move to make sure that she don't smoke a doobie [marijuana cigarette] or crack without him.

Richie's harsh tone reflects the disdain of Shanty residents for Sammy. It reveals as well the kinds of suspicions that plague every relationship in the Shanty. Sammy claims that he accompanies Lisa on the stroll to protect her and make sure she's OK. Richie reads this behavior as spying, as distrust fueled by concerns over drugs and money.

Lisa gave birth while I was at the Shanty. A few days later, after surrendering the baby to social services, Lisa was once again back out on the stroll. When I left the Shanty Sammy and Lisa were still together.

In terms of both the understandings that underlie them and their basic form, relations of friendship and love in the Shanty bear a striking resemblance to those found among the housed population. Several factors no doubt account for this. First, many of the relationships existed prior to the participants' becoming homeless. Second, the privacy afforded by the huts in the Shanty provide a space in which relationships can flourish. And third, the absence of proximate physical dangers diminishes the need for a strong group solidarity, however flawed, that might work against one-on-one relations.

Nevertheless, relations of love and friendship at the Shanty clearly suffer from the stresses of impoverished circumstances and drug addictions. Extreme dependence can foster distrust and with it conflict and disillusionment. Such disillusionment resembles quite closely that observed by anthropologist Elliot Liebow: "The recognition that, at bottom, friendship is not a bigger-than-life relationship is sometimes expressed as a repudiation of all would-be friends ('I don't need you or any other mother-fucker') or as a cynical denial that friendship as a system of mutual aid and support exists at all."[3] Whether such resentment breaks up the relationship depends, of course, on the parties involved. Relationships based on ties made before entering the Shanty or based on love tend to weather the vicissitudes better than others.

PART II

In the Shelters

CHAPTER THREE

More Than Refuge: The Armory

AT THE NORTHERN TIP OF MANHATTAN, across from one of New York's largest hospitals, is an old armory that is home, depending upon the season, to between seven and eight hundred men. The Armory is one of New York City's largest public shelters, run under the authority of the Human Resources Administration (HRA), a municipal agency. Unlike most cities, New York is required by court order to provide shelter for its homeless. A 1981 consent decree, in fact, established a "right to shelter" for men. Subsequent litigation extended this right to women and families and established minimum standards that all shelters are supposed to follow.[1]

"This Place Has No Supervision"

> There are really no rules. They have rules but nobody really enforces them. They try to do their best. People here are drug addicts, alcoholics. A lot of these guys can't even stay in Wards Island [a public shelter] because they can't abide by the rules.
>
> *Dexter*

One enters the Armory after passing through a metal detector and showing identification to guards, who are always on duty. In addition to a guard booth the first floor contains laundry facilities. On the shelter's second floor are bathrooms and showers, the kitchen and dining room, and social service and medical facilities. During the day, many men sit, often for hours, slumped over in chairs, waiting to see doctors or social workers. The second floor also contains a large recreation room. It is no longer in use and remains locked day and night under orders of the shelter's new director. He had the television and VCR once housed in the recreation facility moved to a much smaller room on another floor. Restricting access to television, he hoped, would force the men to use their time more productively. Instead, he made both the men and his superiors at HRA angry. As one resident quipped: "That guy is a knucklehead. Do you see how small his head is? There are almost twelve hundred people in here, and he goin' to make this little room into a TV area. The people came from downtown and told him it wasn't goin' to work." The shelter's third floor is where the action is, where residents spend much of their time, both sleeping and awake. It is a single, undivided drill floor the size of a football field. Approximately seven hundred cots fill this space, lined up one next to the other, row after row after row.

In order to gain entrance into the Armory, or any public shelter for that matter, I had to obtain a "monitor" I.D. card from the New York City Coalition for the Homeless, a legal advocacy and watchdog group. Monitors are supposed to inspect the condition of the shelter and the residents and report back to the Coalition any wrongdoing on the part of the staff. For reasons that will become clear, the Coalition has a difficult time recruiting volunteers to monitor the public shelters. They can be dirty and dangerous.

There are easier pursuits for people wishing to volunteer their time.

I did not want to be a monitor, however. I did not want the residents or the staff to perceive me as anything other than a researcher. Having two roles, such as researcher and monitor, can confuse people and make it harder to gain their trust. The Coalition was sensitive to this dilemma and allowed me to obtain a monitor card without having to be one. We made a deal. I kept them informally appraised of what I saw inside the Armory but had no formal reporting responsibility. I did not identify myself as a monitor to either shelter residents or the staff inside. My card was simply a way, though certainly not foolproof, to get past the guards at the door.

In April of 1989, about two years before I first visited the Armory, HRA instituted significant changes in its public shelter policy. A program of "segmentation" attempted to allocate spaces in various shelters according to individual characteristics or needs. New clients of the shelter system were required to go through a twenty-six-day assessment period after which they would be assigned to a shelter designed to address their needs. The policy created shelters for homeless with jobs, for the mentally ill, for those over forty-five, and for the handicapped. It also designated several shelters as general-purpose facilities—segmented only on the basis of sex—to be open to those who fit none of the above criteria. Concerned with the generalizability of findings from a single-purpose shelter, I decided to sample from a list of general-purpose facilities. I selected the Armory at random from a list provided by the Coalition for the Homeless.

Though it is not officially designated as such, I discovered after some time that the Armory is the shelter of last resort. Residents arrive there after having been processed by social workers who deem them unsuitable for other shelters with segmented populations or after having been thrown out of another shelter for "inappropriate behavior," such as stealing, curfew violation, and other infractions of shelter rules. Anthony and his cousin Clyde, for example, had been staying in Harlem 2, another general-purpose shelter. They thought that they could make some money by selling extra sheets to the residents. They were caught and transferred to the Armory. According to Dexter, "You see a lot of these people can't go to another shelter because they are messed up. If you mess up at a shelter, they don't want you back. They give you a code three [an order of eviction] or something. You know, they just don't want them there no more. They can't put you in the street." Unlike many of the shelters within New York City's public-shelter system, where an individual may be evicted because he breaks a rule, the Armory is designated for rule breakers and others who do not meet the criteria of other public shelters.

I did not know this going into the study—in fact, I learned of the Armory's status and reputation only after spending considerable time there. I had selected a general-purpose shelter at random, and chance placed me in what many consider to be the worst of New York's public shelters. It is possible that, as a result of this decision, I ended up in the most violent and lawless of the shelters. Conversations with homeless people throughout Manhattan, however, suggest that conditions within the Armory are simply an extreme case of those found in other facilities.

Although some residents leave the shelter in warmer seasons, the shelter is almost always full in the winter. Some residents have lived at the Armory for over seven years and others for only a few months. Some leave the Armory for more permanent housing only to return after losing it. Most of the men I met have lived in the Armory on and off for between two and three years.

The experience of Anthony, a black man in his mid- to late twenties, is typical of the off-and-on nature of shelter residence: "I was in here back in '84 and I stayed here for a good seven months. I kind of was tryin' to get myself together and I got welfare and I got out of here within seven months. That was back in '84. Then I started to goof off, gettin' high, and I lost my apartment, lost my job, and I had to come back here." Anthony first became homeless when his father kicked him out of the house because, as Anthony describes it, he "got a bit too confident." He explains:

> I started gettin' high and bringin' girls up there and havin' sex and all that, and it kept goin' on and on and on until one day he just pulled the rope. He said either the crack goes or you go. Well, I said I was goin' to chill and I was goin' to stop, but I went back on my word. He told me one day that he wanted me to go away and not tell him where I was goin' but to just go away. He said that when I come back he wanted to see me a hundred percent better than I was before. I understood where my father was comin' from. I took it to head and said damn, he's right. He didn't tell me to get out; he just told me to go away and get myself together and stop smokin' crack.

Anthony tried to get himself together. He got a job and found an apartment. But he started "goofin' off again" and lost both. He lived with a girlfriend briefly. When that ended, he went to another men's shelter until he was transferred to the Armory. Others have similar tales. Manny's wife allows him to stay with her on weekends. He can stay "permanently" when he can "get his act together," that is, get a job and a steady income. Eggy had just gotten a job as a security guard when I first met him. He remains at the Armory, refusing to go home until he gets his first paycheck. He does not want to be a "burden" on his family. He explains:

> My sister came here with my little nieces and everybody. I wasn't around them for about four weeks, maybe longer. So when she saw me, she hated this, she started to cry. She told me that I don't have to be here, that she had a room for me, that my stepmother had a room for me. But I didn't get paid yet so I don't think I'll go home.

Eggy is torn between not wanting to impose on his family and the difficulty of living in an environment that has "temptations":

> It's not an easy place. I didn't realize it. It's hard for you to move on in life here. The temptation is here, you know. The first thing they see [new residents] is they get three square meals a day; they have a bed, a TV, a job. They can spend their money; they have no responsibility. So I was doin' that for the first two months. I got a place to lie down and eat. I got caught in the mix, you know, gettin' high. Constantly gettin' high. I got no money and I'm fed up with that. There's got to be a better life somewhere. You can never make a life out of here.

For Eggy, Manny, and Anthony, like many others at the Armory, public shelters are part of what might well be considered a repertoire of improvised housing options. Movement in and out of the shelter is consistent with the ebb and flow of the goodwill of family and friends and the vagaries of the itinerant job market. Such repertoires wreak havoc with conventional definitions. Manny, for example, is homeless Monday through Friday but housed on the weekends he spends with his wife. Researchers Kim Hopper and Jim Baumohl describe such circumstances in more general terms: "The more typical picture [of 'the homeless'], that is, is one of chronically makeshift ways of life that occasionally 'fail' and spill over into the official pool of homelessness."[2]

Residents of the Armory receive, as they put it, "three hots and a cot," three meals a day and a place to sleep. Thus these men are not plagued by a constant struggle with hunger, as are those who live in the Station and at the Shanty. By virtue of their contact with the social service personnel who run the facility, most are enrolled in New York State's General Assistance Program. After making allowance for the cost of food and shelter, which is deducted from their checks, benefits total $22.50 every two weeks. One resident, Dexter, told me, "Welfare is a ridiculous predicament. Why waste so much time to collect so little of your benefits? You just become a target because people know when you collect your benefits." Most residents, therefore, attempt to supplement this meager income with various hustles and with whatever itinerant work they can find. Some residents sell books on the street; some sell individual cigarettes to residents too poor to buy a full pack; others panhandle. Given that the material essentials of life are provided for them, money-making efforts are not as all-consuming as in places like the Station and the Shanty, where the homeless "go it alone."

Watching Your Back

Violence is, however, a greater concern for those who live in the Armory than in the other locations I visited. Dexter told me that not long before my first visit, a resident was murdered: "Yeah, they scald a man to death down in the shower the other day. Somehow the shower wasn't workin'. These guys had a beef, and somehow one of them made the water real hot. I don't know how he did it. Scald him to death." Other unconfirmed tales of murder are commonplace, and less severe violence and robbery are virtually daily occurrences. Residents fear not only one another but also the security guards and institutional aides (I.A.'s) who, more than one resident told me, would resort to violence and intimidation in their dealings with shelter clients.

My own experience at the Armory is testament to the intimidating nature of life on the drill floor. Each time I visited the shelter, I would have to fight my way in, explaining to the guards that I had the right to be there. Once inside, I would hear the guard radio to others over the walkie-talkie, "She's on her way up." Guards and I.A.'s would then line the narrow stairwell to the drill floor like a gauntlet, forcing me to press my way through. Making my way past them, I would encounter other guards who stopped whatever they were doing to stare, sometimes whistling, sometimes barking. At times one or another would follow behind me, suggesting that maybe we could "get together." Ignoring these remarks failed. Over time the suggestions became more graphic and the guard's self-professed ability to "make me happy" more exaggerated. I decided to come back at them aggressively. When one security guard suggested that I "suck" his "dick," I told him that he looked limber enough to do it better himself. When another told me that he wanted to "eat my pussy," I asked if this was because his nose was longer than his dick. This toughness earned me the respect of some of the guards as well as residents who overheard the verbal sparring. I was able to come across as neither naive nor easily intimidated. My demeanor was that of a "hard ass." A few resented me more, however. I was warned that people often had "accidents," such as falling down a flight of stairs or finding themselves in the middle of an unexpected brawl between residents. Fortunately for me, at least, no "accidents" ever happened.

Violence, however, is not the only danger that confronts those who live in the Armory. Living in such close quarters makes them susceptible to many contagious diseases. Low-grade infections fester and often blossom into life-threatening illnesses, such as pneumonia and tuberculosis. Throughout my research at the Armory, I had myself tested frequently for tuberculosis. Though the tests were always negative, I was never in good health during my time in the shelter. I had a persistent low-grade fever and cold from which I recovered only after the conclusion of my study.

Perhaps the best indicator of the level of both violence and disease in this and other city shelters is the extent to which many of the homeless avoid them. Testifying in a 1984 New York District Court case, Hopper said that among the homeless who live on the street, between 80 and 85 percent have had some experience in city shelters. Hopper goes onto describe their reasons for not returning to them:

In our research the reasons usually given included personal threat of injury, particularly against the elderly and more disabled, the threat of lice infestation in particular, the threat of robbery, clothes can still be a scarce item on the street, good clothes, and people in the flops that I visited and slept in tended to sleep in their clothes both for reasons of warmth and to make sure they had them when they woke up, and simply for some people they elect to preserve whatever threads of dignity and self-respect are left them rather than submit to what they found to be often a degrading and humiliating experience in the offer of the shelter.[3]

The level of violence in the Armory reflects the limited role of outside authorities in regulating shelter life. The city's Human Resources Administration, which administers the facility, has a list of rules intended to make it a safe and livable place. However, the I.A.'s and security guards who are its de jure custodians rarely, if ever, enforce the rules. According to Anthony:

Half of them do their job; the other half just do shit. They come here and they don't do shit. Like the one here with the earrings, that hussy. She's a real nasty bitch; nobody likes her. And when it comes time to work, she's too tired or her legs and feet hurt. They talk to you like you're a piece of shit because they got a job and they get paid every two weeks, and they talk to you like you're the scum of the earth. It's not very encouraging. They keep downing you and downing you and downing you.

The arrangement of beds on the drill floor is an initial sign of the breakdown of shelter rules. According to the "Operating Standards under the Callahan Decree," they are to be spaced a minimum of three feet apart. In fact, some are three feet apart, others are one or two feet apart, and still others are pushed together. One resident compares the disorder of the Armory with another city shelter, Wards Island, where criteria for admission are stricter and where, unlike at the Armory, it is possible to get kicked out: "This place has no supervision. At Wards Island they have no beds pushed together. At Wards Island when you get up you got to make the bed. Do you see any beds made here? At Wards Island if you don't make your bed you lose it. The people don't care. That's why this place is run like it is because nobody cares." The agents of shelter authority—institutional aides and security guards—are responsible for allocating basic services and supervision in a disinterested manner. They quite simply don't.

This general failure is most acute with respect to the basic exigencies of survival: food and safety. The management of the food line provides an excellent example. Shelter rules require the residents to line up outside the dining area prior to mealtime and wait until the security guards or I.A.'s signal that the meal service has begun. On several occasions I stood in line with the residents or waited inside the dining area until the security guards opened the doors and let them in. On one occasion, one of the residents sneaked into the dining area past two security guards. When I asked one guard why he did nothing, he said, "We are not allowed to have any physical contact with the men unless we're provoked into a fight." The other guard looked over and added, "He's a homo, and you don't want to deal with that shit. He's just too pretty." Guards are similarly circumspect with respect to protecting residents and their property. Each resident has a locker in which he can store personal belongings. Guards do little to safeguard these facilities, and they are frequently broken into. Most men choose to sleep with their most valued belongings, such as sneakers, under their mattresses or clutched in their grasp.

On the Drill Floor

The Armory can be, I learned early in my stay there, a dangerous place. On the vast open drill floor that seven hundred men call home, things can happen. Men get sick; they disappear; they die. The authorities do nothing. Muscles, James, Dexter, Rusty, Candy, Anthony, and the others who live here need allies, other residents they can count on to help them get by and stay safe. They create structure within this open space. They make the shelter more than refuge.

The drill floor is divided by the residents who live on it into distinctive territories. The spatial arrangement of the cots, used by the men during the day for hanging out, reveals social divisions analogous to neighborhoods. There are, for example, a great many "Mo's." "Mo" is shelter slang for men who are transgendered—that is, who dress like women, have breasts, and take female hormones but who are still genitally male. Residents, though not guards, refer to them with feminine pronouns and describe them somewhat colorfully as "chicks with dicks." "Mo's" sleep and hang out in the "uptown" section. (One resident referred to this section as "Motown.") "Downtown" is occupied by other groups. Jamaicans and Africans share one corner. Puerto Ricans and Dominicans have their own space, as do the crew, a group of men who claim to be the governing body in the shelter and who are discussed at greater length below. By shelter rules, those classified by psychiatrists as mentally ill occupy a designated row. This rule, unlike most others, is generally respected. Shelter residents fear the sometimes erratic behavior of the mentally ill and consequently leave them alone. Other researchers have found similar isolation of the mentally ill homeless from the more general homeless population. For example, Snow and Anderson, studying the homeless in Austin, Texas, found that "the mentally ill appear to be outcasts even among outsiders. They are avoided by the homeless as much as possible and they seem to reciprocate in kind."[4]

Territories on the drill floor are jealously guarded as turf. Blacks of American origin are keenly aware that they are not welcome in the space appropriated by the Jamaicans and Africans. As they often do outside the Armory, Jamaicans and Africans here believe that American blacks are uneducated, lazy, and generally lower in status than they are. Jacob, a Nigerian man, frequently expressed the friction and status differences between these two groups. "American blacks know nothing about their African roots. They call themselves African Americans, but they have no education about Africa." Jacob maintains that he is the son of a tribal chief. He talks only to the other Africans and Jamaicans he sleeps closest to. Others, specifically American-born blacks, fall short of his expectations. "I don't trust [them] because they have a disposition that is greedy. They are not generous, nor do they share." For Jacob, survival is predicated on maintaining a "strong character," that is, not getting caught up in a "crowd" that can drag you down and make things difficult in the long run. For him American-born blacks are the wrong "crowd." Such sentiments are returned. According to Anthony: "They [Jamaicans and Africans] nuts, cuckoo. They nut balls. They fight over the smallest little things. They fight among each other. Maybe they native habits?"

In such ways the homeless preserve, create, and emphasize status differentials among themselves. (Recall Ron's avowal that he might be homeless but that he didn't have to look homeless.) Such affirmations of status—referred to by Snow and Anderson as "distancing"[5]—are extremely important in a large environment composed almost exclusively of homeless people. Unlike the Station with its thousands of commuters and the Shanty with its adjoining Chinatown neighborhood, the Armory is, in many respects, a social world unto itself.

Within this social world are two distinctive types of social relations. The first involves extremely close ties, sometimes involving sex between pairs of men who sleep in adjoining or connecting cots. The second is group relationships—that is, affiliations between sets of more than ten men who, as at the Station, can usually be found hanging out together and who, if asked, identify one another as associates. The "Mo's," the Puerto Ricans and Dominicans, the Jamaicans and Africans, and the "crew" are all groups in this sense.

Relations between groups are very different from those at the Station.[6] While the two major cliques at the Station tended to get along, those at the Armory are antagonistic and far more protective of turf and the privileges associated with it. Rico, the Puerto Rican member of the clique at the Station, sometimes associates with members of the Latino clique. At the Armory such associations would not be tolerated. Groups in the Armory fight for control over life in the shelter. In no way did either the clique at the

Station nor the neighbors in the Shanty attempt to control what went on there. In the Armory the fight for power is the most fundamental basis for group life.

The homeless who do not directly participate in such struggles for authority—and they are the majority—survive by developing protective relations with one of the contending groups or with a single and trusted other. For example, Anthony, though not a member of a group, has one strong relationship within the Armory. He spends his time with Milton, whom he credits with helping him beat his addiction. Anthony says, "He told me that the only way to beat cocaine out of your body is to work it out, sweat it out. So I started punchin' the bag and started sweatin' all that poison out. I eventually started gettin' bigger and bigger. When I first came here I was thin as wind. I was real small." Anthony, in fact, is in good physical condition. He is of average height and somewhat muscular. He wears a bandanna around his head or his neck. He recently got himself on welfare. When he is not looking for work, he works out on Nautilus equipment in the Armory and concentrates on staying straight. His maxim for himself and for others is: "You can live in the shelter but you don't have to look like you live in a shelter. You can have a clean-cut face, clean sneakers, clean pants, clean shave, deodorant, clean underwear, the whole bit. You have self-respect for yourself. That's what a lot of guys need is self-respect. Something to lift them up."

Pops, a black man in his late fifties, is older than most of the other Armory residents. Pops spends most of his time when he is not working—he loads and unloads trucks—hanging out in Pigeon Park with James and Rusty, two close friends who will be introduced below. Pops spends little time in the Armory, avoiding as best he can the turf wars and violence that go on inside. Except for his relationship with James and Rusty, he keeps largely to himself, sleeping in a bed next to the guard booth in order to gain whatever small protection such a spot can offer. This particular episode of Pops's homelessness was brief: he had entered the Armory not long before I first visited there, and on my last visit I learned from James that he had found a place to live.

The most successful or powerful group among the competing factions in the Armory is the "crew," also referred to as the "house gang" or "posse." They are my focus. This decision was, in many ways, forced upon me. During my initial visits to the shelter, I spent time with several "crew" members. Subsequent to those early visits, I found members of other groups, as well as unaffiliated individuals, quite hesitant or completely unwilling to talk to me. James, a young black man in his mid-twenties who had lived in the Armory for approximately seven months, told me, after much prodding, that people feared retribution from the "crew." According to James: "Sooner or later it's goin' to get out that you goin' around askin' people questions. . . . You may talk to the wrong person and it would get out that this lady is comin' around askin' questions and shit." Residents not only feared retribution from the crew but also from several security guards and institutional aides who succeeded in intimidating several of the residents from talking to me. During one visit, I spoke to a couple of residents from Nigeria and Jamaica. Afterwards I noticed one of the I.A.'s go over to talk with them. The next day the two men, neither of whom appeared to be busy, told me that they had no time to talk with me. My subsequent attempts to converse with them were equally futile. Other occupants of the "Nigerian and Jamaican section" were similarly reticent. While my focus on the "crew" does not represent the full range of group life in the Armory, all of it is based on the control of territory and the struggle for authority, so that the inner workings of the "crew" are illustrative of these broad dynamics.

The crew's relative willingness to talk with me no doubt stemmed from their position of power within the shelter. As a ruling elite, they clearly had less to fear than others in sharing information with me. I still had to pass muster, however. I had to prove that I was credible. Two factors were important: my authenticity as a female afforded me some security while my ability to stand up for myself earned me some very important respect.

The question of whether I was a "real woman" was an abiding concern. In a social world where conventional sexual categories are blurred and things may not be as they seem, knowing "what" you are talking to is the first step in getting an angle on who you are talking to. Ironically, my somewhat dowdy dress—usually a baggy pair of jeans, T-shirt, baseball cap, and a red winter coat—hinted at my authenticity. I did not exaggerate my femininity by wearing tight dresses and heavy make-up as most of the "Mo's" at the shelter did. Since I put so little effort into "looking like a woman," I had to be "real." Some residents, in fact, made jokes or suggestions, often telling me that I should take a few tips from the "Mo's" and wear tighter clothes or make-up to make me look more "ladylike." One resident even suggested that I "get advice" from the "Mo's" on how to look "like a lady." By showing good humor in these occasions, I helped to open up the lines of communication and began to gain the trust of many of the residents, effects on my ego notwithstanding.

I also had to stand up for myself. I quickly learned that

ignoring certain remarks without challenging them was not advisable. Once I was standing at a table at the far end of the dining room and was surprised when several of the men joined me. One smiled and asked, "Are you going to study all the animals that live here?" I smiled back and said, "I study people, not animals." We both laughed. From the other end of the table, a man, whose name I later learned was Chucky, yelled that I should not have laughed at the remark about animals. He said that when a woman smiles at a man that means that she agrees with him. I told him that it was not true: sometimes a woman smiles at a man because she disagrees with him. I apologized for any insult he had inferred. He exploded, yelling that he should kill me and all the white people in the world. He said that he was prejudiced and that he wanted me dead and that if he couldn't kill me, he would kill my children and drink their blood. Several of the men at the table told him to "chill out." Others just laughed and ignored him. Eventually, he moved to another table, and I began talking to another resident. Then, without warning, an egg hit the man I was speaking with in the head, and Chucky yelled from another table that no one should talk to me. He got angrier and finally stormed out. For the rest of the meal, no one would talk to me.

I realized I had to be more assertive. Rather than backing down as I had in the dining room, I had to meet confrontations head on. I had to demonstrate to the residents, in particular to crew members, that I was neither afraid nor weak. The next morning I had the opportunity. On my way up to the drill floor, I was stopped by five men, including Chucky. They cornered me and Chucky started to badger me with questions about whether or not I was "the one in the line-up." I asked what he meant.

Soon several others implied that I was the "lady in the line-up." Again I asked what they meant. Finally, after much prodding, Chucky informed me that I had given each of them a "blow job" and that I should get on my knees and "suck their dicks" again. Trying to humiliate me, they laughed and joked about my sexual performance. They taunted me with sexually explicit requests as well as insults about my physical appearance. I did not ignore them this time. In a booming voice, loud enough for others to hear, I screamed that under no circumstances was I ever in a line-up with any of them and that none of them could even get a date with a "real woman," no matter how hard they tried. People milling throughout the hallway stopped to watch. Perhaps empowered by an audience, I continued that they had better get used to "sucking each other's dicks" because that was all they were going to get. After what seemed like a decade of silence, a couple of the men told me to "fuck off" and walked away. The others retorted that the only reason that I got so angry was because their charges were true. Then they too walked away.

At the time I was convinced that I had gone too far. I had insulted members of the most powerful group in the Armory. I feared that I would now be the target for more extreme forms of antagonism, possibly even violence. In fact, however, the "line-up" incident was the last time I was actually threatened. Perhaps it was because I was a "real woman." As one resident put it, "If someone was to beat the crap out of you, they would get fucked up because of the simple fact that you is a girl. A real girl." More likely, however, I had demonstrated to the crew members, as well as other residents and the staff, that I could stand up for myself, that I was, in fact, worth talking to.

The Crew

> The Puerto Ricans hang together and the Jamaicans and Africans hang together, but they don't mess with the house gang.
>
> *James*

The "crew" is made up of approximately fifteen American blacks who claim to be a "governing" body within the Armory. In the words of one crew member, "We enforce the rules. Everything that got somethin' to do in here that got a special detail done the house gang will do it." Crew members take it upon themselves to create order in a chaotic environment. As one member boldly explains, "The I.A.'s and the security guards will let anything happen. They will let anything happen. So we got up and got together and formed our own organization in here." The crew attempts to control and administer virtually every aspect of life in the Armory. The crew sets up cots and, to a great extent, decides sleeping arrangements within that portion of the drill floor over which they have control. They also run the food lines into the dining room, provide protection for a price to the many residents of the Armory who lack a group affiliation, distribute over-the-counter medication, decide what shows will be watched on television, and come and go as they please, ignoring the 10:00 P.M. curfew. They also run the Work Employment Program (WEP) line. This program, a fixture in all New York City public shelters, employs a small group of residents in the performance of all routine tasks within the shelter. WEP participants may be called upon to assist in food preparation and clean-up, custodial tasks, and facility maintenance. WEP, however, is not full-time employment and,

in fact, does not inhibit participants from holding jobs outside the shelter.

As the crew see themselves, and as many of the clients
see them, they are a governing body within the Armory.
Their control over shelter life, however, is not complete,
and challenges to their authority from other groups are
common, as the bloodied and frequently swollen face of
the crew leader, Muscles, attests. A black man who is as
physically strong as his name implies, Muscles has a presence that is imposing beyond his physique. He is compact
yet thick; a bald head adds to his no-nonsense appearance.
His bright red sweats make Muscles visible even from the
opposite end of the cavernous drill floor. Crew members
and other residents hold Muscles in esteem. Like leaders in
other contexts, he is seen as someone worth listening to,
strong, intelligent, and able to extend himself in the others' interests:

> Nobody would even think about fuckin' with that
> man. You'll get demoed, you'll get rushed. You will
> get totally fucked up if you fuck with him. Yet he's
> the nicest person you could meet. He will help you
> out if you're a little down and hungry or something;
> if he's got something he'll give it to you. And he's
> running a lot of the house gang.

The crew was formed by a group with long tenure in
the shelter. New members are admitted based on old
members' estimation of their capacity for loyalty and effectiveness. Loyalty is judged according to the prospects'
ability to keep secrets, their tenure in the shelter, and the
quality and character of their personal relations with other
gang members. Effectiveness is judged on the basis of self-

respect and physical strength. Both loyalty and effectiveness are seen as qualities essential to continuing and potentially increasing control of life in the Armory. New members are admitted, after all, with the objective of securing greater power and control.

Members must be able to keep secrets, and several of my questions met fierce resistance. One in particular aroused anger. I was curious to find out what happens to people who "disrespect" crew members by acting like "a big man" or trying to provoke a fight. I wanted to know how crew members sanctioned disrespect. One crew member started to tell me and then abruptly stopped and said, "No, I ain't gonna tell you that; that's too deep. That's too deep for you to know. I might get in trouble for that; that's secret stuff. Then I would have to deal with them [the crew]." Another crew member informed me that there were certain things that he could not talk about because he would get "demoed"—that is, demolished—by other crew members.

Another criterion for membership is tenure in the shelter. The majority of crew members have lived in the Armory on and off for at least three years. Longevity of residence implies that one can be counted on in the future, and it accrues a record, a "resume," a profile of a member or potential member based on experience. One member explained the importance of time to the development of trust between crew members: "If you fuck one of the big guys [from a competing group] up and the niggers [crew members] know you're fighting, then you'll blend in in some kind of way through time. It probably won't work right away, but as you stay here you'll blend in and you'll be down with them." Some crew members have been in the shelter longer than three years. They are, as one member referred to them, "the biggy biggies." They carry more weight than more recent members.

Finally, the quality and character of personal relationships, such as friendship with other crew members, encourages a certain intimacy that ensures loyalty. Sometimes a previous friendship with a crew member or a friend of a crew member is a shortcut into the crew. For example, one recently accepted member, Hugo, was a friend of Richie, who was friends with Calvin, a long-time crew member. He commented: "It was pretty easy for me to get down with the crew, 'cause I knew someone that was down with them for about ten years."

Hugo, twenty-six, is not one of the "biggy biggies" like Muscles, but he is clearly "down with the crew." Hugo is not a large man, nor is he as imposing as Muscles. He is shorter than average and about twenty-five pounds overweight. Hugo has been in the shelter on and off for three years. He prides himself on being a good fighter. That and his affiliation with another long-term crew member secured him a place in the group. According to Hugo, "I got down with the crew when I came here. It was pretty easy for me to get down with the crew because I knew someone that was down with them for about ten years. Plus, you won't get down with them if you're a sucker. You gotta use your hands."

Two qualities contribute to making someone an effective crew member, self-respect and the ability to stand up for oneself. According to some members of the crew, if you respect yourself, then you will be respected by others. Self-respect translates in many ways into the ability to govern, and of course power and the ability to govern can increase an individual's stock of self-respect. One member expressed the idea of self-respect vividly when I asked him about becoming a member of the crew: "Well, let me tell you how the house gang is. The house gang is not bullies and stuff like that. It's people that respect themselves [more] than other clients in here. They [have] more [self-] respect. Their heads is more together so they can get things done, so they can run more things." As in the Station, one way a person can demonstrate self-respect and the ability to govern is to refrain from smoking crack. According to one crew member, "Everybody else in here is so wrapped up in smokin' everyday, smokin' crack. They bringin' theirselves lower and they get smaller and smaller every day. They got no respect for theirselves and if they got no respect for theirself they can't expect to get respect."

Standing up for one's rights is also important. For example, a person first entering the shelter is assigned a bed by shelter administrators. However, these assignments, with the exception of bed assignments for the mentally ill, are rarely permanent. Often residents change their bed assignments in favor of beds located in other sections of the drill floor. One way a resident can demonstrate self-respect, or in fact power, is to take possession of a bed even if the person in the neighboring bed doesn't want him to sleep there:

> Like if you needed a bed and this bed is empty, right. And if I'm here and I tell you that you can't have this bed 'cause it's my man's bed, you got to be thorough enough to not go for it. If you're gonna be thorough enough to say, "Nah, this bed is empty and I need a place to stay and I'm gonna sleep here," that's thorough enough, right. Or [are] you gonna be a wimp and just walk away? That's no respect for yourself.

Self-respect, then, not only requires having your wits about you—that is, not letting yourself "shrivel up" because you smoke crack every day—but also being "thorough" (strong) enough to see conflicts through to the end. Crew members need to be able to back up their words and actions with physical strength and the ability to fight, to be "thorough enough." As one resident put it, "If you can't fight you probably won't get down with them."

"Runnin' It"

Residents of the Armory are supposed to receive, as a matter of right, "three hots [meals] and a cot" and a secure place to live. The breakdown of administrative authority, however, means that they can count on none of these. Much like the men and women at the Station and in the Shanty, they must provide for themselves. In doing so individuals in the crew rely heavily on their personal relations with others. They work together not by sharing or trading but in securing power within the Armory.

The crew is made up of approximately fifteen residents who attempt to control and administer almost every aspect of life in the Armory. As one resident attests, "If a client is runnin' it, he be down with the house gang." In order for the crew to "run" the shelter, the staff must look the other way. Institutional aides and security guards smoke marijuana with the residents. Some have crew members sell drugs for them, both inside and outside the shelter. Their authority is thus compromised. As one crew member suggests: "We got security guards and I.A.'s smokin' with clients. That's how they lose their respect. You see, then we got somethin' over on you. See, we wouldn't be able to run the place without the supervisor, I.A.'s, security guards, without all of them lettin' us." Crew members, in fact, continually "work" their relationships with these authorities—as do members of other groups—to attain power within the Armory. Such effort involves a cooperative effort among crew members to identify and exploit weak spots in the shelter's structure of authority and to present a united front in dealing with them.

The complex trade-offs between shelter staff and the crew resonate with much of the literature on power in prisons. In a summary, researcher Lee Bowker notes that violence and disorder within prisons are often mitigated by "power-sharing factions" among administrators and prisoners. He observes that administrators need to work well with "dominant ethnic groups" and describes how in one prison violence was curbed when the administration "shared power with aggressive Black and syndicate prisoners."[7] The crew, then, "work their relations" with compliant administrators, guards, and I.A.'s. This alliance minimizes the violence between shelter residents while affording specific benefits for crew members.

The crew enjoys privileges other residents are denied. The most important come from controlling the food line and the WEP line. Three times a day the residents queue up at the dining room. It is no surprise that the first in line and the first to eat are members of the crew. In the WEP line, crew members also take their place in the front. According to one crew member, "We run the lines. Who can get in front and who can't get in front. You're supposed to get on in line at the end, but the crew can just walk up in front. Once we get in line, the line goes the right way. The first one in line, the first to get in. After the crew, of course. And if you fight in line, you got to fight us." Running the food line enables them to eat first. Control of the work employment line gets them the best jobs.

Some residents resent the privileges enjoyed by crew members. James, who has lived in the Armory for about six months, spoke bitterly of the crew's food prerogatives: "If you have the privileges, you can go in there and get anything you want. They only let the people in the house gang go past. They said that they was goin' to change it. They said that they were goin' to have the I.A.'s run the food lines and everything. But they said that and they still have the clients runnin' it." Others see these privileges as just payment for the services the crew provide: "They run the line, they have access to the kitchen like it's their own. I don't mind that. I don't mind them runnin' the line 'cause I'm tired of gettin' pushed and stepped on." For this resident, who was not a member of any of the Armory's contending power groups, the protection he receives by being in the good graces of crew members is worth the wait for food.

Crew members protect themselves and create a safer and more predictable environment for themselves and others. Members of the crew, as well as those they are close to, can rely on the support of other crew members in any physical confrontation. To attack one crew member, or to attack a resident who has secured the crew's protection, is to attack all. Crew membership, therefore, provides a strong promise of mutual protection as well as a powerful deterrent seen by others: "You know it's good to have a crew sometimes. Sometimes you might get jumped in here. If they jump me, it's good to know that I can go back there and ask for help and come back with half of the shelter." Challenges to the crew's power by rival groups often force them to fight to maintain their position. But while the threat of intergroup violence is almost constant, crew members and their allies need not fear random and predatory acts of violence—mugging or murder, being beaten, or getting raped. For its members, therefore, the crew in effect rationalizes the violence in the Armory, setting up clear divisions between friends and enemies and mitigating uncertainty.

Like residents of the Station and Shanty, members of the crew use personal relations to provide for themselves, in this case to achieve group power. Unlike what I have described at these other locations, however, this practice is not accompanied by an ethic of self-reliance but rather a clear sense of collective identity and group pride. This identity is expressed in the names the crew give themselves ("house gang," "posse") and also in the use of plural pronouns by themselves and others: "So we got up and got together and formed our own organization in here"; "They run the line, they have access to the kitchen like it's their own."

In the Armory, staying safe in a violent environment is a greater concern than securing resources. Despite the irregularity and incompetence of food provision, it is unlikely that a person living there will go hungry for long. While the privileges extorted by the crew and certain other groups certainly make life more pleasant and indeed profitable, they are not the fundamental reason for the crew's existence. The crew is about protection. Its members and those associated with it believe that it will make them safer. While the men in the Station clique may, on a given day, acquire more resources singly than collectively, the crew clearly and continuously gain by association. In the Station concerns over resource flows and safety are played out against one another; in the Armory concerns about staying alive predominate. The crew is extremely specific with respect to its relations with others. At the Station, outsiders could share if they asked; in the Shanty, the circle of traders includes all who live there; in the Armory, crew members maintain a sharp distinction between allies and everyone else. An unaffiliated person in the Armory cannot simply ask for the crew's help in time of need.

Respect

Mutually recognized rules buttressed with a little terror govern conduct between individuals within the crew. These rules are independent of those of the shelter administrators or those dictated by the crew to outsiders. I asked one crew member to tell me about the group's rules. He responded incredulously, as if the answer were self-evident: "The main rule is respect." "Respect" as they see it is deference to those who have power in their relations with other members; individuals in the crew place paramount importance on the idea of respect. This works two ways. First, individuals expect that others will accord them the respect they deserve. Second, they accord respect to others in their dealings with them. In the Shanty, individuals refrain from pushing their advantage to excess in accordance with a rule that stresses the importance of fairness. In the Armory, crew members restrain themselves from pushing self-interest too far out of concern for the importance of being respected. Pushing too far means losing respect. One crew member explains:

> Some people come in here and play hard, right. They can't do that. They talk tough and try to take over the camp. They think they got muscle or somethin' and

what happens is they get it. I came in with respect. I gave people respect and they liked me. You see, I smoke pot, right. I like weed, right. And I usually buy a lot of weed, right. And when I first came here I started hangin' out with one of my friends, Richie; and he was down with Calvin, and Calvin's pretty big with the house gang. We got to hangin' together a lot and smokin' weed, and they realized how cool I was because I ain't into that rah-rah stuff, you know, big-shot stuff. I just respect everybody and they respect me. I guess they just took a likin' to me and I just went right in, and before I know it, I was just down with everybody, I was down with the crew.

Respect for his fellow crew members, not being into "big-shot stuff" (not being boastful), makes this individual a desirable crew member. He made no demands and broke no rules. Over and above his connections with the "right" people and his ability to supply "weed" (though he is not the only potential supplier in the Armory), his willingness to play by this single, critical rule assures his place in the hierarchy of the crew.

Every crew member must respect every other crew member. Respect is a solidaristic principle, much like that of not "holding out" at the Station. Respect, however, is not owed equally to all crew members. Rather, individuals have earned degrees of respect during their residence at the Armory. Accordingly, before they would talk with me, I had to earn the respect of the crew by not backing down from conflict and standing up for myself. Like one's "word" at the Station, then, respect functions as a reputational device. The leader of the crew, Muscles, has the most. One member explains, "Muscles got all the respect in here in the world." Muscles is due greater levels of deference than anyone else; he has the most power.

Reputations, and consequently respect, are earned through one's experiences in the crew. Much as loyalty and effectiveness are important qualities for the selection of new crew members, so too are they critical for the allocation of respect within the crew. Crew members expect others to treat them in accordance with the amount of respect due them. For Muscles, as well as some of the other senior crew members, high reputations translate into power within the crew. Crew members recognize and abide by a hierarchy:

> I give respect, but I'm not the rough, rough type. You see, in every crew you got your nonviolent type of person. But you keep them around because they cool. They can use their hands and they can fight, but they cool. They don't go pickin' on people. That's kind of what I'm like. Then there are some people that get in closer with the I.A.'s and the supervisors and other stuff that gets you through. That's where a lot of the juice [power] comes from. I got juice, but in the crew there are people that got more weight, more juice than I got.

The rule of respect requires acknowledging one's place within a power hierarchy and not challenging those "that got more weight." As one member warns, "Don't come in acting like a biggy biggy"—that is, don't presume to have more power, respect, and status than you actually have.

While the rule of respect binds individuals to defer to those who have more power than they do, it also constrains those who have "the juice." Because power is built upon respect and because respect is a matter of reputation, individuals who abuse their power, or fail to meet the expectations of others, risk losing the respect on which it is based. According to Whyte: "The man with a low status may violate his obligations without much change in his position. . . . On the other hand, the leader is depended upon by all members to meet his personal obligations. He cannot fail to do so without causing confusion and endangering his position."[8] Were Muscles, for example, to shake down another crew member or fail to come to another's assistance in a dispute, his reputation would suffer and his power diminish.

The crew's power and their ability to use that power to control life in the shelter is based ultimately on physical coercion. Most often it is the threat rather than the execution of violence that musters compliance from the other residents. That the threat of violence from the crew is a deterrent in the Armory became evident when I started to ask question about the crew. Many clients outright refused to answer any questions concerning the crew. Others tried to steer me away. I asked one resident to explain his reticence:

> They may make it difficult. But they would never step on you. But if a person was goin' to get into trouble, they would step on the person that spoke to you. They wouldn't hurt you, but they would step on that person [who spoke to you]. If you were to talk to the wrong person and they were goin' to go up and tell the house gang that you're askin' this and that, the person that you talked to could get into trouble. I don't spill the beans on nobody.

Sometimes, of course, the crew's capacity for violence does need to be demonstrated. Challenges to their power from contending groups, such as the Puerto Ricans, Jamaicans, or Africans, must occasionally be put down with force.

The above discussion might suggest that the crew, especially its highest-ranking members, are capable of doing just about anything they please, but this is not the case. During my many visits to the shelter I neither saw, nor was told of, any instances of random or unprovoked acts of violence nor any episodes of stealing on the part of crew members. Why is it, then, that crew members who seem to have unlimited power stop short of totally abusing that power? Why, given the state of deprivation in which both crew members and residents find themselves, do they not abuse their power for greater material advantage?

Answering these questions requires turning once again to the concept of respect. The shelter would be an impossible place to live if residents had constantly to fear random and unpredictable exertions of power. In order to mitigate this uncertainty, residents need to trust the crew. Residents can trust that crew members will limit their discretionary use of power for fear of losing respect. Respect, as already noted, is based not only on physical strength but also on intelligence and a circumscribed altruism, both of which are subjectively judged. The crew member must be perceived by residents as acting in an intelligent and at least somewhat disinterested manner. If he steals from another resident, he risks losing esteem. Residents may no longer be willing to defer to that crew member in the future. He may, in short, lose power. Respect, then, appears to be a double-edged sword. On one hand, it enables certain residents to achieve a position of power over others; on the other it places clearly defined limits on the exercise of this power, both within and outside the crew. By defining limits, respect mitigates uncertainties. Respect is a de facto contract that is enforced by each resident for the other in the constant process of giving or withholding of respect.

The case of the crew extends our understanding of power relations among the homeless. In sociologist David Wagner's *Checkerboard Square,* residents derived power from their collective resistance to and eventual avoidance of the shelter system.[9] Crew members, however, derive their power from within the shelter. The crew's very existence is contingent upon the social and physical boundaries of the Armory. Lack of administrative authority and lax daily supervision create the conditions under which the crew flourishes. Empowerment is specific to locale. The hierarchy of the crew, delicately constructed around the idea and practice of respect, is similarly not portable. Muscles' respect, earned through long tenure in a particular place, dissolves outside that place. This point is artfully conveyed by sociologist Elijah Anderson in his study of Jelly's, "a hangout for working and nonworking, neighborhood and non-neighborhood Black people, mostly men."[10] Anderson discovered an emergent social order among the "regulars," "wineheads," and "hoodlums," that is predicated on the construction and cultivation of social esteem among peers and limited to those men whose social interaction is continuous and rooted in place—"a place on the corner." The crew, like the "regulars, wineheads, and hoodlums," must negotiate within the narrow parameters of their physical and social space the terms on which respect is constructed and demonstrated. Derived from a constellation of ideas and practices prevailing within a specific location, respect is not a fungible resource. Unlike money, it is extremely valuable in some places and utterly worthless in others.

Rules within the crew are more rigorously enforced than those within the clique at the Station or among neighbors in the Shanty. During my stay at the shelter, I neither witnessed nor heard about any conflict within the crew. While concerns with respect and keeping one's word place the restraint of reputation upon those who live by them, it can be said that acts of disrespect in the crew are much rarer than "holding out" is within the clique at the Station and that they are punished more severely. One merely needs to recall the characterization of Muscles quoted above: "Nobody would even think about fuckin' with that man. You'll get totally demoed. You'll get rushed. You will get totally fucked up if you fuck with him."

Muscles' position as leader is far more unambiguous than that of Ron at the Station. Muscles leads the crew in contending for power in the Armory; Ron tries to keep the peace within the clique. (At the Station, after all, there is nothing to have power over.) A critical difference between the Armory and the Station emerges. "Word" reflects a norm that members of the clique at the Station share with one another; "respect," in the Armory, functions primarily to protect individuals, both in their position within the crew and from outsiders. Protection is much more of an all-or-nothing proposition: either someone comes to your aid—helps you in a fight, defends you against a rival—or not; there is no in-between. Sharing on the other hand tolerates any number of levels of partial compliance. Even if one person doesn't share everything he has, he is still worth having around to the extent that he does share. Respect, the product of a long history of honoring one's commitments, is easily lost forever; no ritualized fight can undo the damage.

Marriage

> They don't have to pay rent here, they don't have to meet
> "real women." All they have to do is push their beds to-
> gether.
>
> *Jacob*

Having addressed the nature of group relations within the crew at the Armory, I now turn to a second type of personal relationship: bonds of trust between pairs of men. The men at the Armory, both in the crew and outside it, tend to pair off. Most can readily identify a single individual with whom they are particularly close. Anthony, good friends with Milton, explains the choice of a partner this way: "Like if you're the type of person who gets high and you know how much you get high, you can find another person who gets high like you do; then you can hang with that person and you can get high together. Now, if you got a job and you want a better job, then you hang with a person with a job better than your job." Unlike at the Station, then, where relationships among group members are undifferentiated, and the Shanty where individuals have multiple relationships, residents of the Armory tend to focus on a single, particular other.

Often these intense pairings become sexual. Just as in prisons, the division of the men into sexual pairs is common in the Armory. According to Anthony, "This is like an outside jail. . . . In a jail you got homos. Same thing they do in jail they do here. This is just like jail. The people in here take it as jail. They put the same image in their mind that they're locked up again. Sometimes it really gets to them because sometimes they do things like they are in jail." Sex on the drill floor and in shower and bathroom stalls is common. For some, like Jacob, the initial shock of seeing men "doing it" in the shower was overwhelming. In the past, prior to entering the Armory, he would have nothing to do with someone who was homosexual. In fact, the first time he saw "it" he ran out of the shower. Now he still thinks sex between men is strange but says he is no longer offended. "You get used to sex in public," confesses Jacob. The lack of privacy does not get in the way. To quote Anthony, "Privacy. Forget it. This is about as private as a football field. But things go on at night." The men speak of partners as "lovers," "husbands," or "wives." Residents often refer to long-term pairs as "married." Any pair of men who appear to residents, security guards, and institutional aides to be particularly intimate or close are assumed (sometimes incorrectly) to be having sex.

The sexual orientation of those in "marriages" varies considerably. Some relationships—particularly those never consummated—are between two "straight" men. Others are between a straight "husband" and a gay "wife." And others are between straight men and "Mo's." Husbands in these relationships see themselves as straight and vigorously assert their heterosexuality despite their relationships with other men. In fact, participants in these marriages do not limit themselves to what can be construed as gender-specific sexual activities. In a practice known to residents and staff as "flipping," for example, the wife takes the dominant position in anal intercourse. Others in the Armory see participants in these marriages as gay. And still others, such as Eggy, see these unions as a response to the scarcity of "real women" in these men's lives. Some, like James, have lovers even though they are unwilling to have sex with them: "I'm not saying that I would never do anything with him or nothin' would ever take place between me and him. But it's just kind of hard for me to get into that because I never done that. It could happen. I love him, I love him more than a friend."

Marriages, neither legally sanctioned nor ritually sealed, offer both material support and protection. Much as husbands and wives in stable society are obligated to come to each other's aid, men in the Armory feel similarly obligated to protect their "spouses." To the extent that the marriage bond is viewed as the human relationship that is most intimate, indissoluble, and infused with trust, some residents enter into marriage, often involving sex, in order to trust.

Consider the kinds of expectations a "Mo" can have of her man, as revealed in a typical event in the shelter. Muscles' "Mo," Candy, was upset by a threatening confrontation with another shelter resident.[11] She sought help from Muscles, who immediately joined the dispute on behalf of Candy. In this particular case, one can say that the sexual bond between the two gave Muscles' "Mo" the certainty that her man would come to her aid.

Being able to count on the support of the man she sleeps with makes a "Mo" powerful and even feared within the shelter. "Some of these homos in here got the biggest juice. These homos got the biggest juice in here," relates Hugo. Like the members of the crew, partners in marriages benefit from the strength and deterrence that their alliances provide.

Marriages also offer material benefit. Many "Mo's" earn incomes from prostitution and from stripping in bars. Anthony explains: "You see, the homos in here has a potential, you know, to go out and get something, you know, money, you know, go out and get a job or find a strip-tease job on Forty-second Street, and they go out there and they make money." Consequently, they have more money, and a more stable flow of money, than the other residents. This makes them desirable as partners for men whose material situation is more precarious.

Much that transpires within marriages can be understood in terms of exchange. The following story comes from Mel, who has lived in the Armory for a couple of years:

> This guy had nothing to do with the gays; he would keep his distance. One day he asked a fag to get him a beer; boom, he got the beer for him. The guy thought that this was great. So the next day he asked him to get him some cigarettes; boom, he got him cigarettes. This guy tried to tell me that this gay guy wasn't so bad. Eventually the gay guy would just give him some money, food, and cigarettes. Boom, the next thing you know he was letting this gay guy suck his dick.

In this story, the exchange seems fairly explicit. Sex is traded for beer, food, and cigarettes, the supply of which is quite unpredictable. Marriages often originate in exchange relations in which sex is initially traded for material goods or protection. Husbands and wives, however, are not simply trading partners. The relationships, and the rules that govern them, go beyond initial and subsequent exchanges to provide a means through which one resident can trust another to act in matters of both exchange and protection.

Those in marriages expect their spouses to behave in ways traditionally sanctioned by the marriage contract. It is taken for granted that an individual will provide for, protect, and in every way look out for his or her spouse. Husbands and wives expect each other to be faithful. Several residents commented that the most vicious fights in the Armory were in response to acts of infidelity—either between "Mo's," one of whom had flirted or had sex with another "Mo's" man, or between husbands and wives.

The case of James and Rusty is typical. When I met James he was lying on his bed shouting that he missed his "wife," Rusty, and was waiting for him to come back from jail. James, a black man in his mid-twenties, and his brother have been in the shelter for approximately six months. James's brother was arrested for selling crack. While his brother was incarcerated, James hooked up with Rusty, a gay white male in his late twenties. James has lived in New York for six and a half years and worked in Brooklyn making mattresses and box springs until he lost his job seven and a half months earlier. According to James, "I came down with the wrong crowd and started smoking crack. I started smokin' crack and then I lost my job. I started smokin' and then I started not goin' to work."

After he lost his job he was unable to pay rent and lost his apartment. He stayed with friends as long as he could, but without a job and with most of his money going to crack, he was unable to pay his share of the rent. Within a month, he found himself homeless and in the worst public shelter in the city. To make matters worse, his addiction to crack grew worse in an environment offering few reasons to abstain. To quote James:

Crack, alcohol, shootin' up, I can understand it. I can understand a lot of people up in here. If you're not used to it, it's a lot of pressure. There's a lot of pressure up in here, and it will make people do things that they really don't want to do. I mean smoke. I remember the first time I came up in here. I was sittin' on my bed with a hundred and fifty dollars in my pocket. I was sittin' here seein' everything that's goin' on, and I said fuck it. I'm gonna get out of here and get a hit, tryin' to relax myself and shit. And after all your money's gone, after which you feel sad and heartbroken and everything, you just say fuck it.

James has not smoked for over five weeks. He is currently looking for steady work. He feels that once he can get work, "something steady, every two weeks," he can get out of the Armory without having to be on welfare.[12]

Consider how James speaks of Rusty, whom, it will be recalled, he calls his "lover" despite the fact that they don't have sex together: "I love him more than a friend. A lover is someone you can really trust and depend on, and that's how I see him. I just don't see him as a friend." Rusty is white and thus somewhat of a target in a predominantly black and Hispanic (Puerto Rican and Dominican) shelter. James protects him: "If someone was to bother him, I would be right by his side." Rusty "boosts"—that is, steals. On a good day, according to James, he can make up to three hundred dollars selling stolen goods. Although the money is good, James wants Rusty to give up boosting. During my time at the Armory, Rusty was arrested for stealing and sent to prison for sixty days. According to James:

I would tell him, "Hey, you is a white person, right. And I know you can get a job quicker than I can." He kept saying that he don't have no identification card, no birth certificate, no Social Security card. But I told him that he could pay for that, send out for that. I kept tellin' him. But that [boosting] was his thing. That was the one thing that he liked doin'.

In his absence, James keeps Rusty's bed intact, his blanket crisp, and his collection of stuffed dolls propped up on pillows. "That's his; nobody can sleep here," he said. Their relationship thus continues even during the separation, both sides bound by the expectation, the trust, that life will resume as it was when Rusty returns to the shelter.

Most marriages, like the relationship between James and Rusty, begin with a simple exchange. Rusty allows James to share in the fruits of his petty thefts—buying him cigarettes and vodka—in return for which James protects Rusty from danger. When, by force of circumstance, the exchange stopped, the relationship did not. James did not replace Rusty even though there were opportunities to do so. Rather, he waited faithfully for his "lover's" return. The trust that had developed through their marriage is not readily dissolved or transferred to another.

Residents in the Armory appropriate and transform the institution of marriage in binding one another with a set of expectations that facilitate trust. Other residents recognize these relations as legitimate and provide sanctions when husbands or wives violate their marriage "contract." Consider how Anthony describes the relationship between Tweetie, a "Mo," and Joe:

Tweetie has a head on her shoulders. That's what he's [Joe] lookin' for. He's lookin' for somebody with a head on their shoulders. She's got welfare and at least some type of potential with herself. The type of potential to get out of here and make a livin' and bring

Joe with her. Joe, he's the type that will get a job and go out there and make some money. This is how they keep themselves goin'. He knows that Tweetie's a man and he still kisses on her and whatever, and it doesn't bother him for the simple reason that she's not bringin' him down and he's not pullin' her down. They not pullin' each other down. It's a kind of bond between them.

In Anthony's words we can see a complete and almost taken-for-granted recognition of the mutual obligations that bind Tweetie and Joe. Anthony speaks of the two in a collective language. Tweetie and Joe are, for him, an inseparable unit. The issue is not whether each will survive individually but how they will "keep themselves goin'." Tweetie and Joe's behavior toward one another is thus subtly, but significantly, constrained by the expectation of their fellow residents, such as Anthony.

Failure to honor spousal commitments, like failure to abide by the requirement of respect, can have reputational consequences. Muscles, for example, is bound to Candy, his "Mo," not only by her expectations but by those of others. People like Anthony recognize the bond that exists between them. For Muscles to treat Candy badly would mean that he is, in general, neither trustworthy nor faithful and might result in a loss of respect. It is easy to see how Candy can place such faith in her husband.

These marriages, like the broader relationships within the crew, are good examples of the use of personal relations in an atmosphere of pervasive distrust. Marriage, at least for some residents, provides universally recognized and legitimated parameters through which one can circumscribe and predict another's future behavior. Thus the idea and practice of fidelity on which these marriages are based play a critical role in mitigating the existential uncertainty of life in the shelter.

But marriages are, like the crew, an imperfect solution. Residents are plagued not only by the tensions of unequal reciprocity—the question "Am I giving more than I am getting?"—but also by the tensions set up by the instrumental origins of the union, the romantic expectations implicit in the ideal of marriage, and the incompatible sexual identities and orientations of the people involved. Many of the straight men would rather be with what they call "a real woman," and many of the "Mo's" know it.

Danny, a twenty-year-old black gay transvestite, has lived in the shelter for two years. Danny has been gay his whole life. He used to work in sales; he began using cocaine and then crack, and then he found himself on the street. According to Danny, "I was so scared when I first came in. I used to just hang out by myself. Eventually I got used to this place. Isn't it strange, to get used to a place like this and get comfortable?" After a while, Danny started to wear makeup and do his nails and hair and wear dresses. Danny claims that he can "be free here." He told me that his lover "came on to me because he really liked my hair." As I talked with them, Danny's lover told me that he would never tell his girlfriend about Danny. He said that he had a six-month-old son and if his girlfriend ever found out about Danny she would kill him. He started laughing and said that no one would know. Danny sat listening, staring straight ahead. A few minutes later I noticed Danny's lover looking at a photograph of a naked woman as Danny fondled him.

Such discrepancies in sexual orientation can also result in tension between the spouses. Rusty wants to sleep with James:

I've known him for a long time, and we haven't even had sex once. He says that he can't because there is not any privacy. So I get up enough money to get a hotel room and James says that he still can't because he's confused. James blames me for confusing him. He said that before he met me, he never even looked at a man. He makes me feel so guilty for doing this to him.

James and Rusty often fight, with James telling Rusty to gather his belongings and move to another section of the drill floor. According to Pops, "Rusty is crazy about James." Unfortunately, James will not consummate the relationship.

As the above incident suggests, relations between husbands and wives are born as much out of necessity as mutual physical attraction. Marriages are a solution to the problems inherent in needing to rely on others in a violent and impoverished environment. Upon entering the Armory one must find an ally quickly. There is no time to discover the kinds of personal qualities in others that facilitate trust. Distrust is addressed by cementing relations in a language where roles and normative behavior are easily understood. Such practices can be contrasted with the way the men at the Station had to monitor one another constantly to prevent cheating or, alternatively, the way those at the Shanty relied on rather traditional gender roles to keep one another in check.

Unlike the clique at the Station, men at the Armory harbor no exaggerated conceptions of friendship. They rely instead on lovers, whom they feel can be trusted more completely and who, as the case of James and Rusty indicates, can be found far more quickly.

The existence of marriage within the Armory echoes findings from other settings with respect to the social construction of kinship. Anthropologist Carol Stack, in her study of poor black women, abandons "widely accepted definitions" of the family for a situationally grounded interpretation that illustrates the material and normative dimensions of family life as it exists in the Flats.[13] Liebow and Anderson explain the underlying obligations that bind individuals together when they are "going for cousins."[14] And sociologist T. D. Moodie, in his analysis of black South African gold-mine workers, discussed the origins, social functions, and ultimate demise of same-sex "mine marriages" in light of proletarianization.[15] Although the socioeconomic, cultural, and historical foundations in which constructed kin relations emerge vary greatly, each of the above examples suggests that monistic understandings of family fail to capture the myriad personal obligations, rights, and commitments that people assign to these socially constructed kin relations. According to sociologists Jaber Gubrium and James Holstein, "Family provides a reference point that is commonly shared and tacitly agreed upon, against which other relationships and behaviors are interpreted."[16] By utilizing the discourse of "family," participants signal to each other and others that their relationship is a personal, nontransferable commitment based on bonds of mutual trust and that it remains, under the most severe circumstances, unassailable.

As in the above examples, the men in the Armory, like Sayjay and Raheem at the Station and Ace at the Shanty, use the language of family when they construct relationships and form alliances. Like the gold miners in South Africa or prison inmates, they pattern their social interactions with one another upon marriage. Marriage provides a common ideology that conveys particular expressions of sexual desire and masculinity and femininity, as well as normative prescriptions that inform husbands and wives of their respective gender roles and of their rights and obligations to one another.

Love relationships in the Armory are similar in many respects to the "buddy" relationships analyzed by sociologist Erving Goffman in his work on total institutions. "The distinctive element about the buddy relation in some total institutions is that it is an exclusively reciprocal relationship (as in the case of the matrimonial relationship): one has but one buddy and one is his only buddy."[17] Yet unlike the relationships Goffman observed, the marriages constructed by the men in the Armory are not, at least in their eyes, their only sexual options. Unlike prison or asylum inmates, Armory residents are not physically confined. I met one man who claimed to maintain a relationship with his girlfriend away from the Armory while simultaneously being a husband inside. Others expressed interest in meeting women, in hooking up with former girlfriends or wives, or in visiting prostitutes. Such talk rarely led to action, however. Though not physically confined to the Armory, the men are, to a great degree, socially confined. Their desirability as mates inside the Armory far exceeds what they experience in the outside world. Their limited potential to get a job and earn a living makes them "unmarriageable" in the sense conveyed by sociologist William Julius Wilson in his analysis of the rise of single parenting and out-of-wedlock births.[18] The Armory makes them "marriageable." They can live up to the prevailing expectations here. As for the members of the crew, husbands and wives owe much of their sense of self to the particular circumstances of the place in which they live.

CHAPTER FOUR

"Stinkin' Thinkin' ": The Private Shelter

LOCATED IN A SMALL ROOM IN THE BACK OF A large New York church is a shelter for no more than ten homeless men, the "Private Shelter." Inside are ten sofabeds. Clean sheets and blankets are stored in unlocked cabinets at one end of the room. Each night the men who live there make up their beds, and each morning, before they leave for the day, they strip them down. At the other end of the room are a bathroom and a small kitchen with a stove, a refrigerator—chained shut when the volunteers go home—and counter space. The bathroom sink is often used to wash vegetables and fruits as well as the large pots and pans used to prepare breakfast and dinner. The walls are yellowed and bare except for several black and red signs announcing that smoking is prohibited.

A Clean and Well-Ordered Place

> This place is pretty good. The men have it pretty together, not like the other shelters, like the Armory. They don't have volunteers; they have guards and case workers.
>
> *James*

The Private Shelter is hard to find. It is accessible only through a parking lot at the side of the church, and there

are no signs to identify it. There is, of course, the ubiqui-
tous guard booth, but unlike at the Armory there are no
metal detectors and no one has an I.D. card. Despite this
fact, I found it the hardest of the four sites I visited to enter. Unlike the Station, Shanty, and the Armory, the Private Shelter is private property; I could claim no right to
be there. It was not surprising, therefore, that on my first
visit, I was not allowed simply to walk in, as I had at the
other places, but rather was referred to the church social
services staff who ran the facility. After I had given them
many assurances of my honest and unobtrusive intentions,
they let me in.

My entrance into the Private Shelter was not dramatic.
No one stopped what they were doing. No one gave me
more than a quick glance. I was neither embraced, as I had
been at the Station and Shanty, nor challenged, as had occurred at the Armory. I was, in fact, ignored. It didn't take
long for me to understand why. The Private Shelter was a
charity dependent on the efforts of volunteers to keep going. The men who lived there saw their fair share of well-
meaning white women every day. There was nothing curious about me.

Used during the day by counselors and social workers for
the church's social services department, the Private Shelter
opens to residents at 7:45 in the evening. Much of the time
before 11:00 P.M. "lights out" is spent preparing and eating
the evening meal and taking turns using the facility's single
shower. Since residents are expected to be out of the shelter
by 7:00 A.M., there simply isn't time for showers in the
morning. Shelter rules prescribe a strict division of labor at
mealtime. On any given evening, one resident is assigned
the task of setting the communal table, which involves
bringing in folding chairs and disposable tableware stored

in the foyer directly outside the shelter. After dinner another resident clears the table and stows the chairs while a third washes the pots and pans. Volunteers do all the cooking; residents are not allowed to cook, one of the volunteers told me, "for sanitary reasons."

Most nights the residents of the Private Shelter eat reasonably well. Meals are usually balanced, nutritious, and even tasty—far superior to the institutionalized fare of large public shelters and soup kitchens. Occasional lapses in the church's food supply are compensated for in ad hoc ways by volunteers. One night Roz, referred to by one of the residents as the "motherly" volunteer, brought chicken and rice she had made at home. Another evening, Deborah brought meatloaf and potatoes. Once, facing the prospect of a fourth consecutive night of spaghetti and tomato sauce, Deborah sent me to the store with her own money to purchase a package of ground beef. Breakfast is a simpler affair, muffins and cereal hastily consumed before the early-morning departure.

There is little truly idle time at the Private Shelter. "By the time we get into the shelter, prepare and eat dinner, make the beds, and shower, there is hardly any time to do anything else," explains Louis, an older resident in his fifties. The routine is, in fact, almost overwhelming. Night after night, the same sequence of well-ordered events unfolds. Strict rules assure it. Residents must be inside the shelter by 8:00 P.M. Once inside, they are not permitted to leave, nor are they allowed visitors. The only thing that changes from one night to the next is the volunteer on duty.

What free time the men do have is generally spent in quiet pursuits. A small foyer outside the main room serves as an informal smoking area. The men often sit in this dimly lighted place—outside the view of the volunteers—sharing cigarettes and conversation. Curtis reviews materials collected at his Alcoholics Anonymous meetings. Others read newspapers, magazines, and comic books. Kevin listens to his Walkman. There used to be a small radio on top of a bookcase in the main room. The volunteers on duty would tune it to a station of their choosing, usually rock and roll. Residents eventually objected. Some wanted a rhythm and blues station. Another wanted news, yet another jazz. Fearing conflict between residents, the radio was removed. For similar reasons there is no television either.

Conflict of any sort is simply not a part of life at the Private Shelter. During my visits I never witnessed anything even resembling an argument between the men who lived there. So peaceful and unthreatening is the environment at the Private Shelter that neither the cabinets in the entryway nor the compartments under the sofabeds—the two places residents are permitted to store their belongings—are locked, and stealing was never a problem.

The men who live in the Private Shelter have it, as James put it, "pretty good." In the context of the unpredictability of the Station, the squalor of the Shanty, and the danger of the Armory, they are—at least in a certain sense—privileged. They are safe and well fed. The place where they sleep is clean, and they do not experience the basic uncertainties that Ron, Susan, and even Muscles are subject to. James, in particular, appreciates such sanctuary. He explains that the Private Shelter protects him from "acid, angel dust, and crack," what he terms the predators of streets and public shelters. A grandfather in his late fifties, James has been "on the streets" since his mother kicked him out of the house—for missing his 9:00 P.M. curfew—when he was thirteen years old. James explains, "I was in a gang. My mother wanted me back at home by 9:00 P.M., but I had to fight or the guys would have beat me up the next day." Ironically, James, who once balked at his mother's 9:00 P.M. curfew, now abides by one equally restrictive. But he says he is no longer enticed by the freedom of the streets: "I'm getting older now, and it's difficult."

Others, however, resent the strict regimen of the Private Shelter, seeing it a trade-off for the material privileges they enjoy. "This place is like a prison," Chris complains, expressing particular bitterness over the Shelter's rigid hours of operation:

> They send you out at 7:00 in the morning rain or shine. They send you out if you are sick. Then what are you supposed to do all day? They will send you out with a fever, when your knees are weak. What are you goin' to do, call the ambulance? They are real strict about getting us out at 7:00 A.M. Only the ones that have clean-up can stay until 7:15 A.M.

Others have a difficult time coping with the lack of privacy in this intimate yet open setting. Unlike the residents of the Station and the Shanty, they cannot "step off the corner" nor close a door for a private moment. According to Al:

> I try to stay out of everybody's way. There's a certain time when we get together, and there's a certain time when we don't. This place is not big enough to go into your own little hiding place. Instead of taking it out on everybody I feel like goin' into my own little hut. But I can't do that, so I have to deal with everybody.

Allen concurs: "Sometimes you just don't want to be fuckin' with anybody, you just don't want nobody around. Sometimes I don't feel like being around here. I just want to get away from everybody. I like my own space. Everybody likes their own space. It's only natural."

Just as the administrators of the Private Shelter closely order the lives of shelter residents while they are on church property, so too do they exert a strong influence on what the men do when they leave the facility. Social service workers at the church are a constant presence. They participate in the initial screening process by which men are admitted to the Shelter. They are vigilant in ensuring that those who are eligible get the welfare payments—General Assistance and, in some cases, Supplemental Security Income (SSI)—to which they are entitled. And they are vigorous in exhorting that during their time away from the Shelter the men should be productive.

The Private Shelter has a mission. It sees itself as a temporary refuge where clients can recover from hard times and, in so doing, escape from homelessness. "We are working primarily with job-bound men: there are no alcohol or drugs," one social worker told me. The idea that the residents must be changed is an important aspect of the institutional culture of this shelter, as it was for the shelters Liebow studied. He writes of one:

> At Bridge House . . . the staff saw themselves as professionals whose job it was to change the women, to help them out of homelessness. They took detailed personal histories, held regular weekly meetings where the women were expected to talk about their problems, developed individual goals for the women in the form of personal contracts (in accordance with the pre-

vailing theories of behavior modification), and held individual evaluation/compliance meetings with the women as needed. For the homeless clients, remaining in the shelter was more or less conditional on fulfilling the terms of one's contract.[1]

The situation is much the same at the Private Shelter. All residents are supposed to be doing something. "Don't expect bums," I was told by social service workers before my first visit.

For some, "being productive" means having a job. Bart is a part-time bookkeeper in an accounting firm. Chris hands out leaflets for a local drugstore. He had a better job, delivering groceries for a midtown deli, but was fired for "wrecking" the delivery bike. Purcell had experienced similar hard luck—he was an elevator repairman until his tools were stolen. His employer refused him either new tools or compensation, so currently he spends his days doing odd jobs around the church—sweeping floors, performing minor repairs, tending the Sunday soup kitchen. Robert also works at the church, running errands for the social services department or cleaning the office. As long as he is "workin' or doin' something," he is allowed to be on church grounds during the day.

Some of the men participate in programs intended to make them more employable. Robert, for example, takes courses preparing him to test for the high school–level General Equivalency Diploma (GED). Black and in his late twenties, Robert is taciturn and spends most of his time doing homework. It was only when I agreed to help him with a math assignment that he agreed to talk to me. Robert had lived in Illinois and came to New York following his release from a mental institution. His family had

had him committed because, he explains, "they thought I was crazy." He lived on the streets for a while and then discovered the Private Shelter during a visit to the church's Sunday soup kitchen:

> Well, I spoke to the guy on Sunday. He told me that on Monday the social services office would be open. This was when it was inside the church itself; now it is in the shelter. But anyway, I went over there Monday and I waited. I interviewed with Father Harrison [the Episcopal priest in charge of the facility], in fact, when I first came into the shelter. He asked me if I was on drugs or alcohol, and I said no.

Robert's commitment to his GED work as well as his helpfulness around the shelter have made him a favorite of the church's social workers. Although stays in the shelter are supposed to be limited to six months, Robert has been there two years.

By far the most popular "productive" activity engaged in by the men in the shelter is rehabilitation from substance abuse. Whether they have a history of alcohol or drug problems or not, residents, according to shelter policy, are expected to refrain from even casual use both in and out of the shelter. Volunteers are told to be alert to signs that a resident had been drinking or had used drugs. Rare violations of curfew are simply assumed to be substance related. Stamping out alcoholism is, shelter social workers explained to me, key to stamping out homelessness.

For those whom social workers have labeled alcoholics, commitment to Alcoholics Anonymous (AA) is expected to be the top priority. Some owe their presence in the shelter to the program. "I came off of a four-month drunk, and my sponsor at AA got me in here," Bart explains. In his late thirties and with a slight build, sandy brown hair, and a mustache, he claims to be a "nasty drunk." When sober he is thoughtful, engaging, and determined, as he puts it, to "get better": "My girlfriend used to hold me while I threw up. One time I was so sick that she called 911, but I ripped the phone out of the wall and kicked it around the room. She left me. She told one of my friends that when I get better she would like to see me." Curtis, for example, has put off looking for work to devote himself full time to his recovery. "Where I'm at in Trinity House [a rehabilitation center], they say you have to at least be there for six months and don't even think about any type of work," he explains. Kevin, in fact, was encouraged by his counselors to give up a twelve-dollar-an-hour job because it conflicted with his AA meetings.

The central role played in shelter life by alcoholism and drug addiction and the prospect of redemption from them is perhaps best illustrated by the case of Curtis. A black man in his mid-thirties, Curtis is completely committed to the philosophy of Alcoholics Anonymous. After an exceptionally destructive binge, Curtis was badly beaten and came to a local social service center for help. He passed through a variety of detox centers, moving from his hometown in New Jersey to upstate New York and eventually to the Private Shelter. According to Curtis, "I just got sick and tired of running the streets, stealing, sleeping in abandoned houses, druggin', you know, those types of things. . . . I really don't know what happened from the day I got high and ended up in upstate New York and eventually here."

Curtis believes that the Private Shelter gives him the "strength and power" not to indulge in "drinkin' and druggin'." In AA fashion, he admits his powerlessness over alcohol and his life. He places his faith and confidence in a "power" that has a greater will than his own. "That high power. To be in the now, to be in the present and live for the present, not for the past, not for the future," he explains. The most important aspect of this power is to allow it into your head, which, as he explains, then forces you to get "out of your head." According to Curtis:

> When you start thinkin', thinkin', that's what we call "stinkin' thinkin'." You think that the so-called good times was when you were out there drinkin' and druggin'. It was no good times. It was misery for me. Misery. I just pray to God that I don't have to go through that anymore. As long as I stay under God he will watch out for me. As far as welfare, I don't have to worry about that because whatever I need he will provide for me. And that's one of the promises that's in the Bible. As long as I stay away from that drink or that drug, everything will go according to his will, not mine, you know. And that's one of the main things, your will. Your will is what gets you drinkin' again. And that's why you have to go by your high power's will. And his will is not for you to drink, is not for you to drug. 'Cause they don't do nothin' for you.

Al tells a different story. "I'm ready to leave New York" were the first words I heard from Al, who recently turned thirty, suffered the end of a relationship, and tested HIV-positive. His frustration and fear were immediately apparent:

> I want my life. I don't have no occupation. I used to cook and things like that, and being gay in the city,

and an ended relationship. I know there are a lot of other things I can pursue in the city, but I want to get out of New York. I don't feel free in New York. I've been here six years now. I'll be thirty, and I just want to change my life around at thirty. I just want to leave the city. That's what I want to do. No one can tell me, not even the program [Alcoholics Anonymous] can tell me what I really want to do now at thirty, even though, you know, I should listen to suggestions.

Al became homeless when his boyfriend abandoned and betrayed him. He had been saving for a trip to Europe, a birthday present to himself. Coming home one day, he found his belongings, money, and lover were gone. On top of that, he had recently tested HIV-positive, a fact he conceals from shelter administrators, volunteers, and fellow residents. Like Curtis, Al spends most of his time attending AA meetings. He does so, he explains, not so much out of commitment to the program as out of a desire to please shelter administrators and occupy empty time.

Al's concern over AA in the face of his grave illness is evidence of the pervasiveness of the shelter's ideology of moral betterment. Al is sick, homeless, and, not surprisingly, depressed. His depression and resignation are misconstrued by volunteers such as Arnold, who encourage Al to "get with the program" [the AA program]. Arnold tries to make himself an example for Al by telling him that things will get better if he throws himself willingly into AA. If it worked for Arnold, it will work for Al. Of course, Al's problems are quite different. The case of Al perhaps demonstrates most clearly the way in which the shelter seeks to transform the material and physical distress of its clients into psychological distress that can be cured by an act of will and the grace of God—in other words, through a twelve-step program such as AA.

"A Gift of Time"

> I expected "dirty people." They're all so clean; you would never know they are homeless.
>
> *Sarah, a volunteer*

At the Station, the Shanty, and the Armory, the composition of groups and the social worlds they inhabit are determined, with some level of autonomy, by the members themselves. The Private Shelter, by contrast, is very much an administered social world set up and run by professionals and volunteers. They decide who can live in the shelter, how long they can stay once they are there, and even what they can and cannot do once inside.

Father Harrison, an Episcopal priest, runs all the church's social services programs and consequently is in charge of the shelter. While lay social workers at the church perform much of the day-to-day administration, all potential residents of the shelter must be approved by Father Harrison. Leon, a lay employee, is responsible for maintaining the facility. As part of this job, he runs the volunteer program, recruiting, supervising, and ostensibly training the individuals who spend their nights at the shelter with the residents. In fact, I learned such training is limited. "They [social services] used to have meetings. Now only about two people show up," Deborah remarked when I asked her how she had been trained.

Volunteers are essential to the shelter's smooth functioning since church staff are rarely present during the facility's hours of operation. Volunteers work, at most, one or two days a week. On some nights there are as many as three volunteers present, on others only one. "There are problems," Father Harrison explained, in recruiting and maintaining a steady corps of volunteers. Deborah, who has been volunteering for over a year, concurred: "They have a hard time getting people to come in." The majority of those who do volunteer are members of the church or students from nearby universities. "They are," as Father Harrison believes, "giving a gift of time."

Most of the volunteers I met expressed a genuine desire to help others. "I wanted to stop feeling guilty," Robin, a college undergraduate explained. Working at the shelter fits in well with her schedule:

> I originally wanted to be a Big Sister. I wanted to take the semester off, but I found out that it was a two-year commitment. Then I wanted to tutor high school kids. But the program was so disorganized. They broke appointments! I even cut my Christmas vacation short a day, and they canceled the meeting! I saw a sign about volunteering on campus. I can only work on Tuesdays.

Kevin came to the shelter much the same way. Nicknamed by residents "The Captain," Kevin is an ex-Marine who joined the church when he started law school. I was there the first night he volunteered. "I used to just drop by, but this is the first night that I'm staying the duration. I have been volunteering since I was thirteen. I used to be a Big Brother, but with law school I had to stop," he told me.

Like Kevin and Robin, Paul is also a student. He feels the shelter gives him perspective. "It keeps me real. I don't want to be a stuffy academic that is not in touch with the world around him," he says. When I met Paul, he had been working on and off at the shelter for about six months. A graduate student in his mid-to-late forties, Paul is clear about what he expects from the residents: "gratitude." "When I started working here they used to be so grateful. They used to share." Now, he complains, "They're not as grateful as they used to be. Remember those muffins that these guys brought in tonight [a charitable donation from a nearby fraternity]? Notice how they didn't share them with the other men. And did you also notice that they [the leftovers] were thrown out?" Without "gratitude" and a willingness to "share," Paul explained to me, the residents would not "make it out of the shelter." Arnold, the only black volunteer I met while I was at the shelter, is "grateful," however. Once a resident himself, Arnold is proud of his change in status. "I came back to give back to the church," he told me. "I was confirmed before I left."

For the most part, volunteers spend their time cooking, serving, and eating dinner and talking with the residents. A shelter administrator described what the volunteers do as "visiting." Janet frequently helps Robert with his math homework. Dana, "one of the better volunteers," according to several residents, jokes around with them. Nights at the shelter when she is on duty are noticeably livelier. Arnold offers himself as a role model, giving advice and urging the men to plan for the future. "Perseverance. I made goals to shoot for, to go for," I watched him tell them on several different occasions. Administrators also attempt to recruit volunteers who are willing to work an eleven-to-seven shift sleeping on a cot in the foyer. Due to a shortage of willing volunteers, this shift often goes unfilled.

The most consequential role played by volunteers is as enforcers of shelter rules. The task of enforcing the facility's strict standards of behavior—its curfews, its prohibitions against drinking and drugs, its expectation that time will be used productively—falls to these unpaid outsiders. In the absence of professional caretakers, volunteers have considerable discretion. Richard explains: "I use the rules if they can help. But if they get in the way of what we are trying to do here, I really don't bother. We are trying to give the men shelter, and if the rules get in the way, then who's going to know? For the most part, I just use my own discretion." Such discretionary enforcement means that the way rules are enforced on a particular night varies according to who is on duty. It varies as well according to how particular volunteers feel about particular residents. Sarah decides how to enforce the rules based on the person she is dealing with: "I really just deal with things as they come along. Sometimes I look at the rules, but I basically make decisions on what I know about the person. If Purcell wanted to talk to friends, I'll usually let him do it because you know Purcell." But others are not given the same latitude; Sarah wouldn't let Chris visit his friend.

Variation in the way rules are enforced between nights and between individual residents leaves some bitter. James, for example, was told he could not take a job he was offered because it would have required him to miss the 8:00 P.M. curfew. Although James welcomes the safer environment of the Private Shelter over that of the street and public shelters, he became "depressed" about having to pass up a job opportunity and stayed away from the shelter for three consecutive nights. When he returned he complained to me, "I'm not treated fairly. The other men are allowed to come back late but I'm not allowed to."

Volunteers not only tell residents what they can and cannot do, they also deal with situations when rules are actually broken. They do not confront residents directly about infractions but rather are encouraged to record incidents in a "logbook" to be reviewed by church social service workers. Volunteers use the logbook to record more general impressions of the residents as well. One week's entries reveal the close scrutiny under which shelter residents live. Different volunteers wrote that "James be brought in line," that is, be made to behave more agreeably; that Edward was using obscenities and "ought to get the help he needs"; and that Chris and Edward had gotten into an argument. Because rule violations are dealt with after the fact, residents rarely have the opportunity to defend their actions. Alicia, the volunteer on duty during Chris and Edward's argument, said nothing to them about it. She waited until the men were preparing for bed to "write up" the incident. Shelter administrators place a great deal of faith in the volunteers and the veracity of what is written in the logbook. Residents, for their part, view the book with a mixture of fear and suspicion. What is written there is the basis not only for scoldings from church social workers but, in the event of either extreme or frequent rule violations, for eviction from the shelter.

Evictions, though not common, are a constant threat in the Private Shelter. All the residents I spoke to knew of at least one person who had been thrown out. Consider Liebow's discussion of the threat of eviction in one shelter he studied:

> What is so striking about these particular incidents is the way some of the staff leaped to suspension/evic-

tion as a proximate rather than ultimate sanction. Here, too, fear played a decisive role. Because staff were often afraid to engage the women one-on-one on the issue at hand, there was little room for negotiation or compromise, or for graduated penalties that attempted to fit the punishment to the crime.[2]

Some rules are unlikely to result in eviction no matter how often they are broken. Proscriptions against smoking in the shelter are an example. Smoking, in fact, was not even prohibited until one of the volunteers complained that the shelter was too smoky. Kevin explains, "I guess it's really not her fault at all. But when we [the residents] spoke to Father Harrison about it, he just said that the church was now going to be a smoke-free place. And so up went the 'No Smoking' signs." Every resident continues to smoke inside the shelter despite the rule. The foyer's designation as a de facto, if not de jure, smoking area is evidence that not all rules are created equal. In marked contrast to the leniency with respect to smoking is the strict enforcement of shelter rules concerning drugs or alcohol. A resident is likely to be dismissed from the Private Shelter if he is caught using, or is suspected of having used, drugs or alcohol even once, whether on or off the premises. Those who perpetually come in late without prior notification, who skip nights, or who cause a disturbance in the shelter may also be made to leave. Interestingly, these misbehaviors are generally assumed in the explanations of volunteers and administrators, and even other residents, to have substance abuse as a root cause.

Several stories indicate the ways in which alcohol comes to serve as a scapegoat for all that goes wrong in the shelter. Carl, who worked in a hospital as an orderly while studying to become a paramedic, often came in around 9:00 P.M., approximately one hour past curfew. He was not thrown out of the shelter until one of the volunteers wrote in the logbook that she smelled alcohol on his breath. Philip's eviction is equally colored. Told by shelter administrators that he had to leave because he spent the weekend with his ex-girlfriend and some other friends and did not come back until Sunday night, Philip claims that he was expelled when he confessed to a resident to having drunk a beer. According to Philip, "We are all treated as alcoholics and drug addicts. Even when we're not, we're treated as such."

Edward's story reveals the extent to which even evictions that appear unrelated to drinking are seen by residents as having alcohol use as their ultimate cause. Deborah, the volunteer who on a previous occasion wrote in the logbook that Edward "ought to get the help that he needs," told me one evening that Edward (whom she described as "the man who babbles") was "thrown out" of the shelter for "touching a volunteer." "I have been trying to get rid of Edward," she told me. "He one time was being very obscene and called me 'Babe.'" Later that evening I asked Bart what happened. His response was similar to Deborah's, that Edward "touched a volunteer." When I told him that I didn't realize that touching volunteers wasn't permitted, he corrected me and said, "No, Edward was goin' off, and got a little crazy with one of the volunteers. He was packing. He was packing a bottle."

"You Are All Guilty"

EDWARD: Who are you?

GWEN: I'm a student writing a research paper for sociology.

EDWARD: Would it be all right for me to say that the field is cursed?

GWEN: How so?

EDWARD: Because it's people like you that made me lose my job. No one should talk to you.

My first meeting with Edward, a resident

For Edward, shelter administrators, volunteers, and sociologists—often and understandably confused with social workers—"are all guilty," all parts of a social work establishment that has come to run his life. Strict rules and unpredictable and occasionally harsh punishments lead others to criticize the church. Philip offers that, "The charity given by the church is not genuine," while Chris confided in hushed tones: "The church has all this money. The church doesn't pay for the shelter, they get the money from the state. The only reason they want you to sign up is so they get the money. They don't even give you food. A shelter should provide you with three meals a day." The shelter is a world very much polarized between caretakers and their clients; it was very difficult for me to stake out independent ground. I too was guilty.

White, middle class, and a student at the nearby university, I was often taken—despite my protests—as a volunteer. One evening early in my research, Chris asked if he could leave for a couple of hours—an infraction of shelter rules—to hand out flyers at the local drugstore. Sarah immediately directed Chris's request to me. I reminded her that I was not a volunteer. Chris grew frustrated by our debate. He told us that he had worked the previous evening. "Check the logbook," he said. Sarah walked away, leaving me to make the final decision. I looked in the book and saw that Chris had indeed been given permission. I let him go. Because I was in the shelter more frequently than any single volunteer, residents looked to me in matters of discretion regardless of whether I wanted them to. "You sound like a broken record, Gwen," Kevin responded in a huff when I told him I was a researcher, not a volunteer. They came to depend on me to know what was going on, to know the rules, and know how they were to be enforced. Given the discretionary nature of rule enforcement at the Private Shelter, the residents looked to me for continuity.

I worked harder to distance myself from the role and activities of the volunteers. I spent less time in the shelter proper, hanging out instead in the foyer, offering the men cigarettes, smoking with them. Yet still I was suspected. The men behaved cautiously with me, and I always felt a quiet tension when I was with them. With Billy that tension became more open.

Billy was new to the Private Shelter, arriving one evening that I was there. He asked me what I did. I told him I was a student and made it clear that I was not one of the volunteers. He asked what I was doing for Easter. I told him that I didn't celebrate Easter. He then told me about "being a Jew and having Christ. Allow Christ into your life. It would make you a lot happier," he suggested. As he was talking, Deborah, the volunteer on duty, looked over. "Bullshit," she mouthed to me. Billy was black and in his mid-thirties. He drove a cab and worked the early morning shift. When he asked Deborah for an alarm clock so he could wake up at 3:30 A.M., Deborah was reluctant. "This is not going to work. He will not be here long," she told me. She recorded his request into the logbook.

Billy referred to himself as "the rabbi." The following evening he lectured the residents throughout dinner on

Martin Luther King and Jesus. In the middle of a lengthy speech, he stopped, turned to me, and asked if I thought I was a "country girl." (I was wearing a pair of blue jeans, a flannel shirt, and cowboy boots.) I laughed and told Billy that I found my attire comfortable. He persisted. "You think you're a country girl," he repeated. "You're built like a football player who thinks they're a country girl." Jack, another resident, asked Billy to be quiet. He kept talking, kept calling me a "country girl."

Bart, Billy, and I remained at the dinner table long after the other residents had left. Bart and I were quietly talking about drinking, relationships, and "getting dumped." Billy interrupted. He said that the way we were talking, we resembled "lovebirds." He moved his chair closer to us and smiled. "I feel something big inside my pants," he shouted. "I ain't getting no attention with the two of you talking." His yelling intensified: "The volunteers the other night were so sweet, and the ones tonight are so awful. The food is crap. You're a country girl who can't get along in the city. You think you're a cowboy with those boots. You think you're so tough." Billy continued to complain about the food, the volunteers, and having to wake up early to get to work. Angry myself, I told him to "be quiet and go to bed." He stopped talking and stared at me. "Are you telling me to shut up?" he yelled. "Are you telling the rabbi to shut up?" I answered, "Yes," got up, and walked away. The residents joined in. "Why don't you just shut up; you're bothering everyone. Just mellow out and go to sleep," Chris yelled from his bed. "Just be quiet," James told him. Bart made faces behind his back. The commotion eventually died down, and Billy went to sleep.

Two nights later I was back in the shelter. I checked the logbook to see how Sarah, the volunteer on duty the night of our confrontation, wrote up the incident. I discovered that, in fact, she had not made an entry for that evening. I discovered as well that Billy had been absent the following night. I asked Chris if he knew where Billy had gone. Just as he was telling me that he did not know, Billy walked in. I had been told that residents who skipped a night were required to show the volunteer on duty a readmittance slip from social services. This rule was in fact written in bold ink on top of the daily attendance roster that residents signed each evening. Melinda, the volunteer on duty that night, didn't read the logbook. She didn't know that Billy hadn't been there the previous evening and so never asked him for his readmittance letter.

I was curious, however. Did Billy know the rules? Did he have a letter? I had already begun to focus on rules as a research question. Outside Melinda's view, I asked Billy if he had a letter of readmittance. Billy misinterpreted my researcher's curiosity for a volunteer's enforcement and responded defensively:

> I'm different. I have a job and I go to school. They know my situation. The people at social services know. They know I work and go to school. Let me tell you how it is. I work and go to school. I'm not like these guys. I am in a very special situation. I gotta do what I have to do to survive. I work and go to school.

I tried to explain the purpose of my question. He just became angrier: "I work; there is no way I could get a letter. I'm different; you don't understand. It's people like you that put me in this situation. You're the bitch that was here the last time. You've had it out for me since the beginning.

You're a Nazi." He threatened me: "You remind me of a white girl from Mississippi. You're going to get yours. You had your chance. It's between you and me. Now I have to go sleep in the subway." Then he quieted: "I am trying to get out of here. I lost my lease. I can't help it if I lost my lease. I am trying to find a home." He turned away from me, grabbed a bag of clothing, and walked out of the shelter. I was stunned. What had happened?

I learned from others that I had, in fact, kicked Billy out of the shelter. What I thought was curiosity had, in fact, been universally understood as enforcement. Some applauded me. "You handled that perfectly. That guy is psychotic. I'm sorry I wimped out, man, but that guy is crazy. You handled it great," said Chris, who had watched the whole incident without getting involved. Melinda expressed relief that Billy was gone. McKinney told me reassuringly that he understood why I had kicked Billy out. "I can see his side of the story too," he confessed:

> Everybody can get a job. But sometimes the rules at the shelter don't help you get a job. Some of the men tell social services that they will be in late, and sometimes social services says it's OK. I would want to talk face to face with Father Harrison so we could discuss things between him and me. But I am not in a position to change the rules.

"I don't get involved in stuff like this," James told me when I asked his opinion. I left that evening feeling extremely guilty and confused.

Thinking about the incident with Billy after it happened, I felt initially that I had failed. I had, I thought, relinquished even the most surface appearance of objectivity; I had forced a homeless man out onto the streets. Upon further reflection, I began to think very differently about the incident. I did not kick Billy out in any kind of deliberate or purposeful way; rather a collection of events—his earlier conflicts with me, my questions regarding his apparent violation of the rules—had come to be defined by him, by other residents, and finally even by me as an eviction. I came to see in my "failure" some very telling truths about this environment. I had had confrontations with homeless people before. It is hard to do the research I do without encountering some antagonism. I always fight back when challenged; not to do so would cause a complete loss of respect among my respondents. But my bark is much worse than my bite. I had not encountered anyone who backed down and retreated the way Billy did. His prompt withdrawal from both the situation and the shelter itself crystallized for me what was truly troubling about the place: the resignation and fear in which its residents live their lives.

My visits to the Private Shelter spanned a two-year period. I spent more time there that at any of the other sites. Through it all, I came to understand the place best in terms of what it lacked: the dignified pride of a Ron, the passionate fidelity of a Susan, the menacing arrogance of a Muscles. The men at the Private Shelter lived in conditions that were materially better and more secure than any of the other homeless people I met. But they had clearly given something up in return.

Whither Friends

> The guys don't really hang tough. They're all too busy doing their own thing. Everybody likes to keep within their own distances. They don't like to conversate. They

don't like to sit and joke and goof around. Everybody
likes to stay isolated.

Curtis, a resident

Although they do not choose the people they live with,
the men at the Private Shelter do derive a sense of group
identity and distinction from living there. Among the
groups I studied—the clique at the Station, neighbors in
the Shanty, and the crew in the Armory—the men in the
Private Shelter show the greatest tendency to see themselves as different from other homeless people.

Their sense of elitism is exhibited by their work at the
church's soup kitchen. On Sundays the residents become
volunteers. Every Sunday the church has a soup kitchen
open to hundreds of homeless men, women, and children. In fact, Sayjay, from the Station, mentioned that
the clique had eaten a meal or two there. This is one of
the few times that the men are allowed on church
grounds beyond the regular shelter hours. According to
Robert:

> On Sundays I volunteer at the Soup Kitchen. I help
> set up the tables and make peanut butter sandwiches.
> There is usually not much to do after that, not unless
> there's a spot in the kitchen. Sometimes I'll try to talk
> to the people, but I don't really have that much to say.
> Hello. Maybe sometimes smoke a cigarette or ask
> them for a cigarette. There's nothin' to rap about.
> You have to know someone to ask them what's hap-
> penin' or somethin'.

Six days a week the men are clients subject to the gov-
ernance of volunteers. On the seventh day, they become

volunteers themselves and administer to the homeless. Such activities require little cooperation or initiative as they are directed by shelter staff. Residents are thus not at the bottom but in the middle of the charitable pecking order. This sustains the distinctions that they make between themselves and the homeless who come to the church's soup kitchen. Robert's explanation that "there's nothin' to rap about" suggests that a common understanding and experience are not shared by all those who are homeless.

Further evidence comes from a homeless man I met one cold night near the church. I asked where he intended to sleep, suggesting that the church might have room for him. He looked at me incredulously, using his hand to turn up his nose to indicate that those who lived at the church looked down on him.

Life for the men in the Private Shelter is different. Procuring food and staying safe—the primary occupations of homeless people in the other three locations—are not immediate concerns here. Starvation, the harsh environment, and violence do not pose a direct threat to the clients of the Private Shelter. Rather, their biggest fear is getting evicted. They have a lot to lose by getting kicked out. They would no longer have a place to sleep at night. They would no longer have a place to shower or store their belongings. They would no longer be guaranteed two decent meals a day. They would lose all stability, certainty, and safety. Getting kicked out would place them in the same position as those who come to the church's Sunday soup kitchen.

One measure of the extent to which the residents fear being kicked out is their unwillingness to discuss the situations of those who have been made to leave. I asked Curtis where Philip went after he left the shelter. He said, "I don't know, I really don't know. He moved, he went back to his lady. I don't know. One day he packed up." Bart dodged my questions concerning Edward's whereabouts after his eviction. "Ed can take care of himself," he casually remarked. Accordingly, when a resident leaves the Private Shelter, he is gone in every sense. The whereabouts of expelled residents are universally unknown. Nobody, to my knowledge, asked; and when I probed, they seemed unwilling to discuss the matter.

Efforts at self-preservation focus on behaving in a manner that shelter volunteers and staff deem appropriate. In the Private Shelter, the clients need to protect their image or standing. They need to remain within the good graces of the shelter volunteers and staff, not other homeless people. They need to cultivate relationships not so much with one another but with individual volunteers and staff members. Such relationships are not easy, given the enormous gap in status between clients and most of the volunteers. Like the staff, the majority are white and middle class, whereas the clients are predominantly black and of course poor.

Many volunteers expect the worst from shelter residents, which places the clients at an immediate disadvantage. Robin told me she was "surprised" that the men at the shelter were not "bums." And consider the following from Paul:

> These guys have no idea about the effect of complex carbohydrates. When you offer them tomato juice, they do not want any. They go for the carbohydrates. . . .
>
> The men here are stuck in a culture of poverty. The culture of poverty is a sociological term that is used to explain the cycle of poverty. . . .

I was walking down the street, and a man asked me for a quarter. I gave him the quarter, and the man said that he really needed two dollars and some change to get some fried rice and chicken wings. I told him that I used to be poor and that he could buy eggs and milk. Basically, he could buy something and stretch it out for a period of two or three days. For these men two dollars is two dollars. They are interested in immediate gratification. That is part of their culture, immediate gratification.

These words are not all that different from the attitudes many New Yorkers express toward the homeless who live among them—a sense that behavioral deficiencies are at the root of homelessness. If the men, in Paul's opinion, could become more sensitive to the fine points of nutrition, if they could "stretch a dollar," they would be better off. "Only two of the men will make it out of the shelter," he told me.

Because Paul and the other volunteers presume that the homeless they tend to are, by virtue of their poverty, behaviorally deficient, and because they see their role as volunteers as teaching better behavior, the burden falls upon individual clients to demonstrate "progress." The men live in a fishbowl, their progress monitored constantly in the logbook by well-meaning volunteers who want their clients to be more like them.

Good relations with individual volunteers are thus critical to maintaining a secure spot within the shelter. Good relations with other clients are, however, not required. Unlike at the other three sites, ties to those with whom one lives do nothing to further survival in the Private Shelter. Ties and obligations to one another can, in fact, be a hindrance. Consider, for example, Chris and James, each of whom accused the other one evening of using drugs and alcohol in the shelter. When Jennifer, one of the volunteers. remarked, "You both sound like you're on drugs," they immediately stopped their bickering and apologized to her, rather than to one another. Residents have nothing to gain but much to lose by disclosing too much information about themselves to other residents. In fact, this information can be used, as the above example suggests, to discredit another resident as well as secure one's own reputation.

If remaining on the good side of shelter staff and volunteers is essential for survival, then relationships with other residents—especially those who may drink, stay out beyond curfew, or are otherwise unfortunate enough to be viewed negatively by the volunteers—can work against you. Being found guilty by association of breaking the rules is a powerful and, given the volunteers' disposition, a reasonable fear. You may not break a rule, but the person you associate with may. What's more, the fear that residents may "snitch" on each other to the volunteers also works against openness between shelter residents. It is, in short, best to keep to yourself. According to Curtis:

> Well, I try to talk. I be goofin' off sometimes. It seems like the guys here have an attitude. I don't know how their day be goin' but my day goes good so that's why I be tryin' to goof off. I be goofin' and they be on the serious side. Like they don't want to hear it, you know, they want to isolate, you know. That's what the men are here. They like to isolate theirselves. I don't know why.

Ties with other residents, therefore, cannot help but might well hurt.

Isolation, as Curtis puts it, is the surest and most appropriate survival strategy in the Private Shelter. By keeping their distance from one another, the clients seek to distinguish themselves in the eyes of volunteers and staff. Much as they distance themselves from those who visit the church's soup kitchen, so too do they distance themselves from one another. Social relationships among the homeless here, unlike at the other three sites, do not help the clients of the Private Shelter get by.

By the time the men arrive in the evening, shower, eat, and settle comfortably for the night, they are too tired to get into "good conversations" and "good communication," as Curtis and Al put it, with the other residents. Even at dinner, conversation is at a minimum, and residents are often strained for topics of conversation. The men talk more with the volunteers than with other residents. When the men do talk to one another, it is usually about the meal and, on rare occasions, current events. Some of the men even skip dinner and remain on their beds, either reading, listening to their Walkmans, or sleeping. The men rarely enter into personal and intimate conversations with other residents. When they do, discussion usually centers around the particular "program" they are involved in or a conversation they recently had with Father Harrison or another shelter administrator. The men, as Curtis suggests, are not interested in one another but rather in their own affairs: "You know, hi and bye, that's enough, I guess. I don't know; I would like to get closer, but most of the men in here are in their own little thing."

Conforming to the Private Shelter's rules that strictly control each resident's activities and behaviors, the men are reticent to talk about themselves, fearful that they may, in one way or another, implicate themselves in situations that could meet with the disapproval of a volunteer and get them kicked out. After all, Philip was kicked out of the Private Shelter after telling another resident that he had spent the weekend with his girlfriend and had a few drinks.

Not only does the Private Shelter constrain social relations within the shelter but it also limits those between residents and outsiders. Residents are not allowed to come in late, which limits their ability to spend time with friends or lovers at the end of the day. They are also not allowed to have visitors. Even at the Armory, where residents are required to show identification before entering, I met a few people, either inside the building or directly outside, who were visiting friends. At the Private Shelter, residents are not even permitted to entertain a visitor outside the building on church grounds. Chris, for example, was furious with both a volunteer and a security guard for not allowing him to spend time with his friend outside the shelter. The security guard was adamant about visitors, claiming that it was against the rules. The volunteer initially agreed to allow the visitor in but later told me that if she allowed one resident to have a visitor, then she would have to allow the others to have visitors as well. She claimed that this would be too much of a "hassle" and lead to too much confusion.

Some constraints on outside friendships, however, are not a consequence of strict shelter policies. Some residents find that it is difficult, even impossible, for them to tell their friends that they are homeless. According to Lewis, fifty-one, "From what I've heard, most people don't want their friends to know that they're homeless, at least most of the guys I've talked to. I guess it would be kind of embarrassing to have a friend in his apartment and you in the street." Allen, forty-eight, refuses to tell his musician friends that he lives in a shelter. The abundant negative stereotypes applied to the homeless lead many of those I met to keep quiet about their status. Even though Lewis argues that "there is no shame if you can't pay your rent," he refuses to tell his daughter that he is homeless. "Homelessness is like wearing a cowbell around your neck," Bart told me.

Some of the men let go of past friendships, often blaming their friends for making them homeless. Al, for example, in response to his lover's abandonment, has rejected his old friends, citing their penchant for drugs and alcohol as his primary reason for avoiding them. According to Al:

> I don't deal with my friends. Everybody is smoking crack. They will drag you down, yes, they will drag you down faster. So I don't deal with them. I will say hi, bye. I'm trying to love myself because I helped out so many people, you know. My lover ran out on me after he got into a motorcycle accident, and I took time out to take care of him the whole week. When he came back [from the hospital], he ran out on me with three thousand dollars of mine and went to Mexico and shit, and now I'm out on the fucking street.

Curtis, who refuses to stay in touch with his old neighborhood friends, comments, "I have a lot of friends on that block, and I know when they see me they [will] say 'Curt, come on, let's go hang out for a while,' you know, and no tellin' what that will lead up to." Curtis, who is in the early stages of his "sobriety," fears that his neighborhood friends will drag him down. The directors of his AA "program," Curtis told me, suggest that he remain sober for ninety days before he "can even think about going back" to his old neighborhood and his friends.

Wary of one another and of those they used to know, the residents of the Private Shelter are left to socialize with those in their "programs." Both Kevin and Curtis socialize during the day with members of their respective AA programs. Kevin plays softball with a group of men from his program. Curtis hangs out with several members of his AA group; they take time between meetings to talk with one another about "sobriety." Robert often spends time studying with other students in his GED course. In all three cases, such friendships are "productive."

PART III

From a Distance

CHAPTER FIVE

Conclusion

"WHAT ARE YOU LOOKING FOR?" A STRANGER asked me as I looked down from the cement wall at what was now an empty space.

"Nothing," I told him.

All that remained of the Shanty was the sturdy chain-link fence. Waist-high weeds, broken bottles, and spent candy wrappers litter the earth where Ace, Sammy, Susan, and the others used to live. On August 17, 1993, city bull-dozers tore down the huts; the plot of land seemed smaller without them. I found the spot where Louie and Susan had buried their dead cats. They were no doubt still there.

Life in the other places I visited had changed as well. In keeping with the spirit of the age, the Armory was down-sized in 1992. It is currently home to only two hundred men, and control of the facility has been transferred to a private agency. My Coalition for the Homeless monitor badge would not get me in. I had to rely on the word of an administrator, who told me excitedly about how the place had improved. "You wouldn't believe it. It looks like a hospital it is so clean," he said over the phone. The flow of life at the Station is much the same as when I first visited there. The faces have changed, however. There were, I discovered, new cliques, new nicknames. People remembered Ron, Sayjay, and Rico, but no one knew what had happened to them. A woman named Pat sang me the chorus of "Get Off the Crack." Even at the Private Shelter, things had changed. Father Harrison was at a new church, where, the shelter's current director told me, "he's happier." Leon "had some problems" and was fired. Residents are currently allowed inside the Shelter two hours earlier in the evening. "It gives them a little more time to socialize," the new director explained to me.

Going back to the places I had visited, I found none of the residents I had met. What had happened to them? Had they moved on to other street communities, other shelters, other shantytowns? Had they secured more stable housing? Were they even still alive? In my abortive attempt to get back into the Armory, I met Dr. Sylvester, a staff psychiatrist with whom I had tangled during my fieldwork there. "There's a nostalgia I feel. It's not like I want things to go back to the way they were, but it's like you go through it and you survive all the chaos. It's important to document things the way they were," he told me. Nostalgia. If the people I met ever escaped their daily struggle to survive, would they feel nostalgia? Would Susan take her daughter—if she ever had one—to see where she had once lived? Would she tell her about Ace, about Ginger, about John, whose name she used to scribble frantically in the dirt? How would Ron or James or Curtis reconstruct their pasts?

Framing the Question

> As they appropriated spaces in railroad stations, subways, lobbies, and doorways, homeless people redefined urban space. They might not be helped, but they could not be ignored.
>
> *Michael Katz*, The Undeserving Poor

The trials and struggles of the people I met are, of course, not only the stuff of personal life histories but also components of a larger public policy debate about homelessness. The past two decades have seen a manifold increase in the incidence, scope, and visibility of homelessness as a social problem. Scholars, journalists, and politicians have engaged in an extensive discourse largely focused on answering the question of cause. Why is it, the question goes, that so many individuals have come to find themselves lacking "customary and regular access to a conventional dwelling."[1] Many blame individuals for their lack of a home. Seizing upon the proportionately higher incidence of mental illness and substance addiction among the homeless, writers like Alice Baum and Donald Burnes have seen such personal problems as principal causes for this social problem: "What we saw . . . were people frustrated and angered by personal lives out of control. They were entrapped by alcohol and drug addictions, mental illness, lack of education and skills, and self-esteem so low it was often manifested as hate."[2] The prominence of mental illness and substance abuse in the popular understanding of homelessness has led to a focus on deviance rather than on poverty. "For whatever sad reason, some people do drift beyond the outer realm of society and never come back," notes President Bill Clinton.[3]

Others have countered with an understanding of homelessness that places the blame on larger structures in the economy and society. Linking the increased numbers of homeless to changes in the political economy of housing— shrinking labor markets, the destruction of low-cost housing in the inner cities—they seek to refute the cultural understandings of homelessness by focusing on circumstances clearly outside the control of individuals.[4] Rather than examine whether the assumptions about the homeless are accurate, they seek to reframe the discussion to emphasize the simple economics of housing in America. Urban planner Peter Marcuse argues forcefully, "Changes in the level of homelessness arise either from decreases in the supply or increases in the demand for housing of the relevant type."[5]

In his highly touted book, *The Homeless,* sociologist Christopher Jencks attempts to forge a much-needed synthesis between the cultural and structural understandings of homelessness. He argues, on one hand, that such factors as changes in the labor market and the destruction of skid row have contributed to an increase in the number of homeless. However, he argues that individual failings—mental illness, substance abuse, poor social skills—are also important aspects of the problem. His approach is captured in the following excerpt:

> In the case of homelessness, conservatives want to blame the homeless, while liberals want to blame the conservatives. Both explanations are correct. If no one drank, took drugs, lost contact with reality, or messed up at work, homelessness would be rare. If America had a safety net comparable to Sweden's or Germany's, homelessness would be rare. It is this combination of personal vulnerability and political indifference that has left people in the streets.[6]

Recognizing correctly that much discussion of the homeless centers on the issue of blame, Jencks seeks to replace the "either-or approach to blame with a both-and approach."[7]

Debate over the causes of homelessness persists in the wake of Jencks's book and no doubt will continue in the years ahead. Fueling the discussion is a premise shared by most participants: if we understood what made people homeless, we could do something about it. Those who stress personal pathology cry for therapy, tough love, and moral contracts to be entered into in exchange for a leg up. Those who stress economic dislocation clamor for more housing, more jobs, more support for those at the dangerous bottom of the economic ladder. Like pragmatic social scientists, individuals on both sides seek to treat the problem by attacking its causes.

This book contributes virtually nothing to the debate about what makes individuals homeless. While specific circumstances that I have recounted can—and no doubt will—be taken by interested parties on all sides as support for their particular positions, such is not my intent. I am not concerned with how certain unfortunate individuals end up homeless but rather with how such an event is in fact the beginning of a dynamic process of living without "regular access to conventional dwelling." Homelessness is a social problem that has not only causes but also consequences. In the most tragic of cases, these consequences are fairly straightforward: they die. But for those who don't, the consequences of homelessness are still quite significant. Homelessness transforms the lives of those who experience it. Below I explore what the places I visited tell us about how it does so and why understanding the effects of homelessness is as critical to forging possible solutions to the problem as is knowledge of its causes.

Places Not Called Home

> Home is shelter that not only provides physical adequacy as shelter, but also privacy, personal safety, security of occupancy, comfort, space for essential resi-

dential activities (varying both historically and with the individual, but typically including in the United States today cooking, eating, sleeping, child raising, tending to personal affairs, and social interaction both within the household and with outsiders), control of the immediate environment, and accessibility, all within a neighborhood that permits the home to fulfill its functions. It involves a set of relationships between a person and his or her housing that supports a deeply felt (and socially conditioned) feeling of identity, belonging, security.

Peter Marcuse, "Homelessness and Housing Policy"

Homelessness is about improvisation. Lacking "conventional" or "customary" dwellings, the homeless find or create shelter in unconventional places—on street corners adjoining bus stations, on empty lots, in shelters of one type or another. As physical structures, these places are not designed for such purposes. Making them habitable, to the extent that they are so, requires continuous effort. At its core, in one form or another, homelessness is a process of constructing shelter where it was not meant to be.

Some of this effort is simply physical work—salvaging cardboard crates to soften the hard terminal floor; repairing one's hut following the inevitable damage of a bad storm; remaining vigilant regarding the whereabouts of all one's earthly possessions; repeating the regimen of nightly chores before 11:00 P.M. "lights out." Any kind of shelter requires some form of maintenance, of course. It is not the physical work that makes the experience of homelessness transforming. It is the social construction of shelter, a process common to all four locations I visited, that makes homelessness distinctive.

The homeless I met survive through their personal relationships. Shared understandings and collective activity turn street corners, empty lots, and unused common rooms into places to live. In making such a claim, I do not mean to argue that there is a "culture of homelessness," that homelessness as a social fact produces a set of beliefs, values, or understandings that transcend particular locations and circumstances and that can be seen—depending on one's political perspective—as empowering and subversive or self-perpetuating and dysfunctional. I argue rather that homelessness encourages a process in which personal relationships are mobilized in the production of what the physical environment fails to provide: a safe and secure place to live. The beliefs, values, and understandings that emerge from this process are situationally specific and local in nature.

So much for the homeless depends on relationships. At the Station and at the Shanty relationships between the homeless residents are critical to securing the material resources needed to survive. At the Station as well as at the Armory relationships among residents are essential to creating—to the extent it is possible—a safe and secure environment. And at all four locations, relationships with representatives of outside authorities—police, public administrators, private social workers—are required to create a "security of occupancy" that residents of conventional housing take for granted.

Basic subsistence is a constant concern at the Station and at the Shanty. Meals and medicine that come free in the shelters must be procured on the streets. Matters are worse for those with drug or alcohol addictions. Friends, lovers, associates—daily companions of various kinds—call upon each other for help almost constantly. They share. They trade. One way or another, critical resources flow along with daily gossip, small talk, and occasional intimacies through almost every relationship.

The velocity with which goods change hands on the streets creates a thicket of obligations. There is no universal code of solidarity among the homeless, no brotherhood or sisterhood of those without homes. Acts of altruism are no more or less common than they are for those who have conventional shelter. Rather, specific rules bind specific individuals to specific standards of behavior. Obligations to be honest in sharing or fair in trading are created by and apply to particular people in particular places. Such local dependencies are not, of course, without problems. Individuals fear that they are being "held out on," that any kindness will be "taken for weakness," that calls for aid are prompted by "wants" and not "needs." Distrust and suspicion between close companions is an inevitable result of a fundamental truth: homelessness transforms personal relationships into the principal currency of survival.

This currency buys more than material things: it can buy safety as well. While Shanty residents feel relatively safe inside their huts and Private Shelter residents know that nothing will happen to them inside the church, those at the Station and at the Armory, with good reason, fear the violence characteristic of their environments. They need protection, and they use their personal relationships to get it. Crew members, clique members, and spouses all watch each other's backs. Alliances forged through group membership and marriage bring with them the obligation to treat an attack on a part as an attack on the whole.

The use of private alliances to secure a safe living space requires that these personal relationships have a public face. Potential adversaries need to know who—that is, how many—they are dealing with and be deterred accordingly. In a closed environment like the Armory, visible declarations of love and fidelity let outsiders know who is with whom. In an open space like the Station, where there are always new outsiders, constant companionship is the only certain way to achieve any strength in numbers. In both cases, the transformation of personal relationships into a means of protection exposes these relationships to wide scrutiny, turning private conduct into the subject of public judgment. Everyone knows just how loyal you are. Obligations become binding both from within and without.

But good relations with other homeless people are not enough. In all four places I visited, outside authorities ultimately had the final say on who could stay and who had to leave. The extent to which the homeless experience outside authority as a threat to their "security of occupancy" varies in seriousness and degree by location. Being told to move along by a beat cop at the Station is of course less grave than having your home demolished by a city bulldozer; the rarity of an Armory eviction is less feared than the common expulsions from the Private Shelter. These differences notwithstanding, people in all four places attempted to cultivate relationships with those who had power over them. Much as they do not expect altruism from one another, they do not expect it from those charged with taking care of them either. Sociologist Herbert Gans writes: "Caretaking is not an altruistic act, but a reciprocal relationship in which the caretaker gives his services in exchange for material or non-material return. The doctor receives a fee; the social worker, deference."[8] It pays to get to know the local beat cop, to co-opt the shelter guard, to be in the good graces of the volunteer. To the extent that such power becomes personalized, it can be made less arbitrary, less unpredictable, and even—or at least so the hope goes—less severe.

In thinking about the places I visited I am tempted to focus on their physical characteristics—the terrifying openness of the Station, the squalor of the Shanty, the warehouselike quality of the Armory drill floor, the complete lack of privacy of the Private Shelter. It is, after all, the structural inadequacy of these places as shelter that brings us to view homelessness as a problem and to feel sympathy for those who endure it. There is more to these places than their physical form, however. Each is a social environment as well. Each survives through the give and take of human relationships, many of which are deeply important to those involved. Each is an example of the ways in which what is physically lacking can be, albeit quite imperfectly, socially constructed.

The Choices They Make

> [Jencks believes that] we can explain and predict people's behavior by comparing their decisions to a universal standard of rationality, and we can find that standard by looking inside ourselves and how we think.
>
> Deborah Stone, "Helter Shelter"

What then can be done? What can a journey into the lives of the homeless, such as this one, tell those who would try to do something about the problem? I return to Jencks's book. Central to his approach to ending homelessness is the question of choice. For Jencks, all individuals have choices. Misfortune, a bad job market, an abusive family situation, or poverty may make the choices available to the homeless far more constrained than those available to most Americans. But the homeless, in Jencks's view, "make choices, like everyone else."[9] Homelessness persists when individuals are presented with a poor set of choices and when they choose badly from those options available to them. One of the principle choices the homeless make, according to Jencks, is between alcohol or drugs and shelter:

> If they do not crave caffeine, nicotine, alcohol, cocaine, they can in principle spend a very large fraction of their cash on rent. . . . People's choices are almost as variable when they can spend $10 a day as when they can spend $1000. . . . Whether he [the drug user] rents a room will depend on how he assesses the trade-off between cocaine and shelter on a particular night.[10]

Jencks's belief in the power of choice, in fact, is sufficiently strong that he goes so far as to suggest that the provision of public shelter may actually have increased the number of individuals we consider homeless. Solving homelessness, he argues, will involve both altering the choices available to the homeless and encouraging them to make their choices differently.

Jencks is wise to direct policy makers' attention to the preferences of those they wish to serve. He fails, however, in his attempt to capture what those preferences are. Jencks's analysis of choice among the homeless rests on two assumptions. He assumes first that the choices he identifies accurately reflect those available to and experienced by the homeless. "We badly need more reliable information on where the homeless get their money and how they spend it," he concedes.[11] He assumes as well that in making choices, the homeless behave as isolated actors, unconstrained and unaffected by their relationships with others. Are food, rent, and drugs the real trade-offs experienced by the homeless? Are the homeless really free agents, unfettered in their ability to make the choices we want them to? The answer to both questions, at least in the places I visited, is no.

The homeless I met did not make choices about where to spend particular nights; they chose instead where to spend stretches of time. While none of these choices are aptly labeled "permanent," the people who make them differ greatly in their time horizons from the prototype offered by Jencks. Shanty dwelling, street life at a bus station, and residence in a public or private shelter are all long-term survival options for those without conventional homes. Different people choose different places. Virtually everyone I met had had some experience in a public shelter. Muscles and Anthony chose to stay; Sayjay and Ace decided to live elsewhere. Sayjay told me that the street was safer than the shelters. A Nigerian man I met at the Armory disagreed. "At least if you are sick, they would find you," he said.

Relationships are important as well. Other people influence the choices the homeless make concerning where to live. Prior affiliations are particularly important in places that present barriers to entry. Many residents of the Private Shelter gained entrance through the efforts of AA sponsors, social workers, and church members who decided to help. The opportunity to live at the Shanty for many residents was based on having a friend or acquaintance who already lived there. Ace knew Red, a Shanty resident, for many years prior to moving there. Sammy came to the Shanty through his girlfriend, Lisa, who already lived there. Susan and John used drugs in the Shanty with some of the residents before actually living there themselves.

The types of relationships one can experience in a particular place are also important factors in the choice of where to live. The Armory, for example, facilitates social relationships and organizations—"gangs" and same-sex marriages—similar in many respects to those commonly found in prisons. It is not surprising, therefore, that many of its residents, including gang leader Muscles, are ex-convicts skilled at surviving in this type of environment. The Private Shelter is best suited to those who are comfortable working with social workers and therapists, while the Shanty is the only place I visited where monogamous heterosexual relationships could flourish.

Much as they influence one's choice of living envrironment so too do personal relationships structure other choices as well. As individuals, the people I met clearly wanted to escape homelessness at some time in the future. As participants in relationships rich in obligations and expectations, however, they directed most of their daily activity at sustaining and surviving their present situations. Most of the time, the people I met chose to do what those closest to them expected. At the Station, clique members shied away from individual economic pursuits that might harm the group. In the Armory, crew members worked to gain and maintain power inside the institution rather than seek advancement outside of it. At the Shanty, using barter rather than cash contributed to economic vitality within the community but did not create value that was negotiable outside. At the Private Shelter, the desire to demonstrate moral improvement to the staff—the prioritization of Alcoholics Anonymous over paid employment—deemphasizes the sheer dollar-and-cents reality of what it takes to get out of homelessness.

These choices make sense. Economic life among the homeless is far more complex than Jencks suggests. Understandings of financial obligations and of use and exchange values, and ultimately decisions on how to allocate meager resources, are all the product of local circumstances and social networks. Rarely are choices a "trade off between cocaine and shelter," as Jencks would lead us to believe. A far more common trade-off is that between permanent allies and temporary housing. At the Station, for example, clique members who "hold out" are not only sanctioned but risk losing more long-term support. A night in a rooming house or cubicle hotel is, in fact, a poor choice compared with its most common alternative: sharing five dollars with the group. Neighbors in the Shanty are better off in the flexible market they have created for themselves than in the more expensive and less yielding market of the outside world. Spending six hours at an Alcoholics Anonymous meeting may purchase far more in the form of caretaker good will in the Private Shelter than the same six hours spent doing itinerant labor. In all these cases, an understanding of the social environment in which the homeless live leads us to see the choices they make as both rational and appropriate. There may be solitary homeless people making the daily "wrong" choice of oblivion over shelter. I haven't met any.

Jencks is right to raise the issue of choice. He is right to suggest that the issue for policy makers is as much how to get the homeless to housing as it is how to get housing to the homeless. He fails, however, because he views the homeless exclusively in terms of what they lack—conventional shelter. I found no hobo adventure, no beatnik freedom, no cause for envy on the streets of New York. The homeless are desperately poor. The conditions in which they live are hard for many even to contemplate. They still have something left to lose, however. The lives they have improvised in the empty spaces of our public world are meaningful, complicated, and consuming. The relationships they engage in are sources of satisfaction and anguish, of security and uncertainty. It is in the context of what they have, not what they lack, that those who seek to improve their circumstances must provide solutions.

I am not a policy expert. I have no magic-bullet solution to the problem of homelessness. I write, however, with the conviction that those who make policy need to understand as best they can the people at whom their programs are directed. This book in no way completes the challenge of documenting the myriad circumstances in which those without homes live. I hope others will join the mission and help to do so.

Notes and Index

NOTES

Chapter One: "Your Word Is Your Bond": The Station

1. Peter Rossi, *Down and Out in America: The Origins of Homelessness* (Chicago: University of Chicago Press, 1989), p. 196.

2. For a discussion of the eligibility of homeless individuals for welfare benefits in New York City, see Brendan O'Flaherty, *Making Room: The Economics of Homelessness* (Cambridge, Mass.: Harvard University Press, 1996), pp. 209–25.

3. In an informal survey of daytime street people in New York City conducted by Columbia University undergraduates in 1993, 42 percent of the respondents—mostly single males—said they were receiving public assistance. Those who slept in missions, shelters, and hotels, to name a few indoor settings, were twice as likely to receive public assistance as those who lived in the streets or who doubled up with friends or relatives. See O'Flaherty, *Making Room,* p. 87. Although my own data reflect a much smaller number receiving public assistance both on and off the streets, more systematic research needs to be done on the numbers of homeless who actually collect some form of public assistance, the factors that deter many who are qualified from collecting benefits, and the real value of these benefits in permitting access to affordable *and* safe housing.

4. Rossi, *Down and Out in America,* p. 186.

5. Saskia Sassen-Koob, "New York City's Informal Economy," in *The Informal Economy: Studies in Advanced and Less Developed Countries,* ed. Alejandro Portes, Manuel Castells, and Lauren A. Benton (Baltimore: Johns Hopkins University Press, 1989), p. 63.

6. David A. Snow and Leon Anderson, *Down on Their Luck: A Study of Homeless Street People* (Berkeley: University of California Press, 1993), p. 146.

7. See ibid., pp. 145–70, for Snow and Anderson's discussion of shadow work. It is difficult to determine the extent to which variance between their findings and mine are the product of the different populations studied (Austin, Texas, vs. New York City) or of different research styles (see especially p. 146, n. 2).

8. Egon Bittner, "The Police on Skid-Row: A Study of Peace Keeping," *American Sociological Review* 32 (1967): 699–715.

9. "Visiting," a term coined by Herbert Gans (personal communication), combines conventional participant observation with a great deal of informal interviewing and probing. Probing—gentle questioning after people make statements—includes phrases such as "What do you mean?" "I don't understand," and my favorite, "Huh?"

10. The term "effortless sociability" comes from Josephine Klein, *Samples from English Cultures,* 2 vols. (London: Routledge and Kegan Paul, 1965), 1: 142, and is cited in Elliot Liebow, *Tally's Corner: A Study of Negro Streetcorner Men* (Boston: Little, Brown and Company, 1967), p. 22, n. 14.

11. The research findings on panhandling and physical appearance are divided. Gmelch and Gmelch and Febrega found that beggars and panhandlers in Ireland and Mexico, respectively, cultivated a disheveled appearance in order to muster sympathy and support from passers-by. In his study of panhandlers at Yale, Goldstein, on the other hand, found that panhandlers tried to maintain a "clean appearance when they panhandled." See George Gmelch and Sharon B. Gmelch, "Begging in Dublin: The Strategies of a Marginal Urban Occupation," *Urban Life* 6 (1978): 439–54; Horatio Febrega, "Begging in a Southeastern Mexican City," *Human Organization* 30 (1971): 277–85; and Brandt Goldstein, "Panhandlers at Yale: An Empirical Study of Panhandling in New Haven, Connecticut" (Yale University Law School, 1992), p. 50. The men in the clique have adopted the former strategy.

12. Goldstein, "Panhandlers at Yale," p. 50.

13. Guy Oakes, *The Soul of a Salesman: The Moral Ethos of Per-*

sonal Sales (Atlantic Highlands, N.J.: Humanities Press International, 1990).

14. Mark Granovetter, "The Strength of Weak Ties," *American Journal of Sociology* 78 (1973): 1360–80.

15. Buying a cup of coffee, a slice of pizza, or a sandwich was a practice I followed throughout my research. I chose this strategy for two reasons. First, I thought that if I gave money to one or two people, I would be asked for money every time I came to the Station; I clearly could not afford this. Second, buying someone a cup of coffee, for example, allowed me to sit down and spend some time talking to the person in relative privacy.

16. As Carol Stack found at the Flats, "Survival demands the sacrifice of upward mobility and geographic movement." See Carol B. Stack, *All Our Kin: Strategies for Survival in a Black Community* (New York: Harper and Row, 1974), p. 125.

17. Compare Ron's appraisal of his leadership qualities with that of Doc, the leader of a group of urban Italian American teenagers: "It wasn't just the punch. I was the one who always thought of the things to do. I was the one with half a brain." See William Foote Whyte, *Street Corner Society: The Social Structure of the Italian Slum* (Chicago: University of Chicago Press, 1943), p. 4.

18. Gerald Suttles, *The Social Order of the Slum: Ethnicity and Territory in the Inner City* (Chicago: University of Chicago Press, 1968), p. 231.

19. Gypsy's words resemble those of the characters Omar and El Raheem in Miguel Pinero's play "Short Eyes," which deals with life among prisoners:

> OMAR: I can't give you my word on something like that. You know I don't stand for no lame coming out the side of his neck with me [lying]. Not my word . . . My word is bond.
> EL RAHEEM: Bond is life.
> OMAR: That's why I can't give you my word. My word is my bond. Man in prison ain't got nothing but his word,

and he's got to be careful who and how and for what he give it for. But I'll tell you this, I'll try to be cool.

See Miguel Pinero, "Short Eyes" (New York: Hill and Wang, 1974), p. 13.

20. *Damien: Omen II* is a 1978 Hollywood film about a child possessed by the devil.

21. Whyte, *Street Corner Society,* p. 258.

22. Carl Cohen, "Social Ties and Friendship Patterns of Old Homeless Men," in *Older Adult Friendship: Structure and Process,* ed. Rebecca Adams and Rose Bliezner (Newbury Park, Calif: Sage, 1989), pp. 222–42.

Chapter Two: "Kindness for Weakness": The Shanty

1. Elliot Liebow found a similar sentiment among homeless women. According to Liebow, "This generalized readiness to be helpful was ever-present, along with a generalized readiness for hostility." See Elliot Liebow, *Tell Them Who I Am: The Lives of Homeless Women* (New York: Free Press, 1993), p. 169.

2. Compare Susan's understanding to that of a sociological account of middle class friendship: "Friends can quite legitimately make use of one another in instrumental ways without threatening the relationship, provided that it is clear that they are being used because they are friends and not friends because they are useful." See Graham A. Allan, *A Sociology of Friendship and Kinship* (Boston: Allen and Unwin, 1979), pp. 34–35.

3. Elliot Liebow, *Tally's Corner: A Study of Negro Streetcorner Men* (Boston: Little, Brown and Company, 1967), p. 180.

Chapter Three: More Than Refuge: The Armory

1. Rulings stemmed from a 1979 class-action lawsuit (Callahan v. Carey) filed by the Coalition for the Homeless on behalf of "derelicts" who could not get into shelters.

2. Kim Hopper and Jim Baumohl, "Held in Abeyance: Rethinking Homelessness and Advocacy," *American Behavioral Scientist* 37 (1994): 527.

3. Marthaann E. Pitts v. Robert S. Black, No. 84 Civ. 5270 (MJL), United States District Court Southern District of New York (1984), p. 6—Transcripts.

4. David A. Snow and Leon Anderson, *Down on Their Luck: A Study of Homeless Street People* (Berkeley: University of California Press, 1993), p. 68.

5. Snow and Anderson report two types of what they refer to as "distancing": "disassociation from the homeless as a general social category, and disassociation from specific groupings of homeless individuals" (ibid., p. 215).

6. The discussion here is confined to the description of differences between groups. Speculation as to the causes of these differences as well as other differences between sites is treated fully in the final chapter.

7. Lee H. Bowker, *Prisoner Subculture* (Lexington, Mass.: Lexington Books, 1977), p. 114.

8. William Foote Whyte, *Street Corner Society: The Social Structure of the Italian Slum* (Chicago: University of Chicago Press, 1943), p. 257.

9. David Wagner, *Checkerboard Square: Culture and Resistance in a Homeless Community* (Boulder, Colo.: Westview Press, 1993).

10. Elijah Anderson, *A Place on the Corner* (Chicago: University of Chicago Press, 1976), p. 1.

11. Several crew members had "spouses" in the Armory. There were no instances, however, of "marriages" between crew members.

12. "Every two weeks" refers to a paycheck.

13. Carol B. Stack, *All Our Kin: Strategies for Survival in a Black Community* (New York: Harper and Row, 1974), p. 31.

14. Elliot Liebow, *Tally's Corner: A Study of Negro Streetcorner Men* (Boston: Little, Brown and Company, 1967), and Anderson, *A Place on the Corner*.

INDEX

AA. *See* Alcoholics Anonymous, and the Private Shelter

Ace, 67, 73, 74, 188, 198; drug use by, 87, 89–90; and friendship, 86, 87, 89–91, 148; home of, 51, 56, 57, 187; on Jimmy, 97; moneymaking by, 59, 67; and Sammy, 80, 85; and sharing, 72, 75; and Susan, 96; and trading, 78, 85

Africans, 114, 115–16, 122, 135

Al, 155, 160–62, 180, 182

Alcoholics Anonymous, and the Private Shelter, 154, 158–59, 161, 162, 182, 200

alcoholism: and the Private Shelter, 158–59 (*see also* Alcoholics Anonymous, and the Private Shelter); in the Shanty, 64, 193; at the Station, 193. *See also* drugs

Alicia, 166

Allen, 156, 181–82

American blacks, 115–16

Anderson, Elijah, 136

Anderson, Leon, 9, 115, 116, 148, 206n. 7, 209n. 5

Angel, 22, 23–24

Anthony, 109, 114, 198; and the Armory, 106, 107–8, 112, 116, 138; on Mo's, 140–41, 144–45; on pri-

vacy, 139; relationship of, with Milton, 117, 138

Armory, 151, 152, 196, 198; author's experiences at, 104–5, 110–11, 118–21, 188; downsizing of, 187; drill floor divided at, 114–16; drug use at, 99, 107, 117, 127, 132, 142; guards at, 103–4, 112, 113–14, 127–28; as last resort, 105–6, 113; marriage at (*see* marriage); meals and bed provided at, 108, 109, 127; moneymaking by residents of, 109–10; relationships at, 116, 119, 138–49, 162, 175, 193, 194–95, 196, 199, 209n. 6; residents of, 106–7; violence and lawlessness at, 103, 106, 110–14, 130, 154, 194

Arnold, 161, 164

authorities, 10–11, 12, 65, 193. 195. *See also* public assistance

Bart, 157, 158–59, 171, 182; on Edward's eviction, 168, 177

Baum, Alice, 189

Baumohl, Jim, 109

Bellevue Men's Shelter, 67